WHO AND WHEN?

The 18th CENTURY

Artists, Writers, and Composers

WHO AND WHEN?

The 18th CENTURY

Artists, Writers, and Composers

Edited by Sarah Halliwell

RSVP

RAINTREE
STECK-VAUGHN
PUBLISHERS
The Steck-Vaughn Company

Austin, Texas

Steck-Vaughn Company

First published 1998 by Raintree Steck-Vaughn Publishers,
an imprint of Steck-Vaughn Company.
Copyright © 1998 Marshall Cavendish Limited.

Library of Congress Cataloging-in-Publication Data
The 18th century: artists, writers, and composers/edited by Sarah Halliwell
p. cm. -- (Who and When: v. 3)
Includes bibliographical references and index.
Summary: Introduces some of the major artists, writers, and composers that flourished
in Europe during the eighteenth century.
ISBN 0-8172-4727-0
1. Arts, Modern -- 18th century -- Juvenile literature. 2. Artists -- Biography -- Juvenile literature.
[1. Arts, Modern -- 18th century. 2. Artists. 3. Authors. 4. Composers]
I. Halliwell, Sarah. II. Series.
NX452.A18 1998
700'.9'033--dc21   97-11620
                                                                                  CIP
                                                                                  AC

Printed and bound in Italy
1 2 3 4 5 6 7 8 9 0 LE 02 01 00 99 98 97

Marshall Cavendish Limited
Managing Editor: Ellen Dupont
Project Editor: Sarah Halliwell
Senior Editor: Andrew Brown
Senior Designer: Richard Newport
Designer: Richard Shiner
Picture administrator: Vimu Patel
Production: Craig Chubb
Index: Ella J. Skene

Raintree Steck-Vaughn
Publishing Director: Walter Kossmann
Project Manager: Joyce Spicer
Editor: Shirley Shalit

Consultants:
Anthea Peppin, National Gallery, London;
Dr. Andrew Hadfield, University of Wales;
Jonathan Kulp, University of Texas.

Contributors:
Andrew Brown, Ian Chilvers, Iain Zaczek,
Ann Kay, Alice Peebles.

CONTENTS

INTRODUCTION

The 18th century conjures up two contrasting images. On the one hand, it was a time of great taste and elegance, when painting, writing, and music reached new heights of sophistication. On the other hand, it is known as the Age of Reason, when people began to question traditional values. These doubts were to bring about dramatic social, political, and artistic changes in the later years of the century.

At first, the main emphasis in the arts was on grace and beauty. Orchestral music became more popular, and the symphony and concerto became established as new musical forms. In painting, artists established the fashionable Rococo style. This was lighthearted, almost to the point of frivolity. Artists such as Jean-Antoine Watteau and Jean-Honoré Fragonard (*see pages 8 and 30*) portrayed the leisured classes at play, strolling about their sumptuous estates, listening to music, and falling in love. The upper classes also liked to purchase other types of picture. They hired artists such as Angelica Kauffmann (*see page 46*) to help decorate their luxurious homes. And wealthy young gentlemen—the first tourists—bought Canaletto's views of Venice to remind them of their travels in Italy (*see page 12*).

For sheer elegance, such artworks have few equals. Yet they present a remarkably narrow picture of the age that created them. Throughout the first two-thirds of the century, most of the major European nations were involved in a series of punishing wars. But these conflicts rarely featured in the art of the period. Eventually, there was a backlash against this mood of escapism. In its place there was a growing taste for pictures with serious themes. These generally depicted historical scenes, which featured great acts of heroism or illustrated a moral tale. Among the leading artists in this field were John Singleton Copley and Benjamin West (*see pages 34 and 40*), the first American artists to become famous in Europe.

The works of these painters were large and impressive. But others preferred to put across their moral lesson in a different way. William Hogarth (*see page 16*), for example, worked on a smaller scale, and injected both humor and sharp social criticism into his scenes. Many of these resembled the political cartoons that can be found in modern newspapers. Hogarth wanted his pictures to reach a wide audience. So he made small printed copies of them, which he could then sell cheaply. Hogarth's critical attitude to authority was echoed by the writers of his time. Daniel

Defoe, Jonathan Swift, and Voltaire (*see pages 58, 62, and 66*) all published satirical novels, which focused on the problems of the period. Today, people consider works such as *Robinson Crusoe* and *Gulliver's Travels* as children's books, but really they were serious moral fables, making criticisms of the society in which the authors lived. The increase in the number of people who could read, and the availability of cheaper books, meant that ideas of this kind spread more quickly and carried greater force. As a result, people began to question the power of their leaders, and to demand new rights and freedoms.

One common concern shared by artists and many others, was the question of work. During the course of the 18th century, painters and composers gradually took greater control of their own careers. Watteau, for example, was one of the first artists to choose the subjects of his pictures, rather than simply obeying the orders of his clients, while Hogarth campaigned for the introduction of a copyright law, preventing other artists from pirating, or copying, his work.

For musicians, the changes were even more fundamental. George Frideric Handel and Joseph Haydn (*see pages 78 and 82*) followed the traditional pattern of seeking a position at court, while Antonio Vivaldi and Johann Sebastian Bach (*see pages 70 and 74*) supported themselves through teaching. Increasingly, though, there was a tendency for composers to work freelance, earning their money from public concerts and the sale of their music. Wolfgang Amadeus Mozart (*see page 86*) was one composer who struggled to make a living in this fashion.

Without doubt, the quest for liberty had its greatest impact in the political arena. The American War of Independence, which began in 1776, was an early consequence of the upsurge of democratic feeling. In Europe, the greatest upheaval was the French Revolution. Under the influence of controversial writers such as Voltaire, and the provocative paintings of Jacques-Louis David (*see page 52*), the rebellion broke out in 1789. The revolutionaries executed King Louis XVI in 1793, and, for a time, France descended into chaos, with many of the original rebels following the king to the guillotine. David was nearly among them, but managed to survive, and pledged his loyalty to the rising star of French politics, Napoleon Bonaparte, who would lead Europe into the modern age.

JEAN-ANTOINE WATTEAU

A fiercely independent spirit, Watteau pioneered a new type of painting. His supremely refined works show elegant lovers playfully enjoying themselves, but all his works are pervaded by a sense of sadness.

Jean-Antoine Watteau was born in October 1684 in Valenciennes, a town in northern France close to the border with Flanders. His father wasted no time in setting his son to work and, at the age of 11, the boy was sent to train under a local artist. Watteau never completed the course, since his father stopped paying the fees. He continued his training with a different painter, however. In 1702, his new master took him to Paris, where he abandoned him.

AN IMPORTANT TEACHER

In Paris, Watteau worked as an assistant to Claude Gillot, an artist who produced theater pictures. Gillot passed on his love of the stage to his pupil. He took Watteau to the Paris street fairs, where he could enjoy the antics of the "Italian Comedy." This was a famous troupe of actors, most of whom wore masks or brightly colored costumes. They presented a mixture of acrobatics, music, and comedy, and also mimed stories about the difficulties of being young and in love. Watteau was enchanted by their performances and began painting them.

Watteau's association with Gillot ended in 1707, when the two men quarreled. Watteau was an irritable, short-tempered man, and often argued with his friends and employers. This may have been due to his tuberculosis, the lung disease that afflicted him for many years, and eventually killed him.

He was moody and impatient. He sometimes spoiled his paintings by rushing them. Worse still, he might even destroy them in a fit of depression. Sirois, one of his picture-dealers, was always fearful when Watteau was nearing the end of a work. "If he finishes it," he told a friend, "it will be his masterpiece; but if bad moods … take hold of him, that will be the end of it."

Watteau's friends were rarely offended by his unpredictable behavior,

Jean-Antoine Watteau, 1721,
by Rosalba Carriera
This delicate pastel portrait shows the artist shortly before his death at 37.

The Scale of Love, c.1715, by Jean-Antoine Watteau
Fashionable people making music together was one of Watteau's favorite themes for his
fêtes galantes. **The two main figures also appear in several other works by the artist.**

however. Despite their quarrel, Gillot even recommended him to his next employer, Claude Audran. As well as being a successful decorative artist, Audran was also in charge of the royal art collection in the Luxembourg Palace in Paris. In the days before public galleries were available, it was important for young artists to gain access to private collections, so that they could improve their skills. At the Luxembourg Palace, Watteau admired the paintings of Peter Paul Rubens, the famous 17th-century Flemish artist. He made many sketches of the pictures, and absorbed Rubens's rich colors into his own style.

INDEPENDENT SPIRIT
Watteau's character brought him an unusual degree of independence. At the time, most artists either worked to order—painting a subject that their

client had chosen for them—or else produced a work from a well-defined category of picture, such as a still life or a landscape. Watteau rarely worked this way, however, preferring to choose his own themes.

OFFICIAL RECOGNITION

In 1712, Watteau applied to be an associate member of the French Royal Academy of Painting, the highest art institute in the land. He was accepted at once. But, like all new associate members of the academy, he had to present a work known as his reception piece before becoming a full member. The academy was so impressed by his skill that it took the unusual step of allowing him to select the subject of his reception piece. Watteau chose the *Pilgrimage to the Island of Cythera*, which showed a group of lovers leaving Cythera, the island associated with Venus, the goddess of love.

A NEW KIND OF ART

Normally, an associate member presented his reception piece to the academy within two years, but Watteau took five years to complete his picture. When the *Pilgrimage* was finally presented in 1717, it was unlike any other previous work and it earned a new classification in the academy—the *fête galante*, meaning courtship party.

For most of his remaining career, Watteau concentrated on *fêtes galantes*. He showed elegant couples enjoying themselves in beautiful woods and parks. They talk, flirt, dance, and serenade each other with music. Some of these works have elements of pure fantasy, such as statues that turn around to listen to the lovers' conversations.

But, even in such a paradise, there is an air of sadness. It is as if the figures are aware that their pleasures cannot last. In part, this may reflect the artist's own illness and fear that his life would be cut short. But it also has something to do with his unusual working method. Instead of making a detailed plan for his pictures, Watteau assembled his figures from several unconnected drawings. This approach had the effect of making them appear isolated and lonely.

Much of Watteau's success was due to the support of Pierre Crozat, a wealthy banker who bought many of his paintings. In his final years, Watteau was also helped by Edmé Gersaint, a close friend and picture-dealer.

The artist's last great work was a marvelous signboard, painted for Gersaint's shop. This huge picture was much more realistic than Watteau's previous work, and hinted at new directions in his work. Sadly, it was all too late. Watteau died in Gersaint's arms on July 18, 1721, at the age of 37.

MAJOR WORKS

c.1715	THE SCALE OF LOVE
1717	PILGRIMAGE TO THE ISLAND OF CYTHERA
c.1718	ACTORS OF THE ITALIAN COMEDY
c.1719	GILLES
1721	GERSAINT'S SIGNBOARD

CANALETTO

The most famous Venetian painter of the 18th century, Canaletto is known for his views of his native city. His precise and detailed works captured the essence of the city and were immensely popular with tourists.

Giovanni Antonio Canal, known as Canaletto—the "little canal"—was born in the north Italian city of Venice on October 28, 1697. His father, Bernardo Canal, was a painter of stage scenery, and the young Giovanni became his assistant. Together they worked on scenery for several operas, including those of the famous Venetian composer, Antonio Vivaldi (*see page 70*).

THE INFLUENCE OF ROME

In about 1720, the father and son visited Rome to work in the opera houses. The architecture of Rome enchanted Canaletto, and he made sketch after sketch of the city's most famous buildings and ancient monuments.

The experience had a profound effect on the young man. After returning to Venice, he gave up working for the theater, and turned instead to painting views of the city, a form of art that was increasingly popular at the time.

At first, he liked to paint the intimate, everyday scenes of traffic on the canals.

He was not afraid to show this "real" Venice. He painted what he saw with great freshness and deep feeling for the watery atmosphere of the city. Soon, however, he was producing more spectacular views, using stronger colors and brighter light. In 1725, a Venetian art dealer wrote of Canaletto's work: "You can see the sun shining in it...."

CHANGING A SCENE

Canaletto painted his canvases in his studio from drawings he had made outside. Although he paid careful attention to the most minute details, he often reorganized or distorted the objects in his paintings to make more striking compositions. He would alter the curve of a canal, for example, or even shift a building to a different position.

Despite these distortions, Canaletto's pictures look almost as accurate and as

Self-portrait, c.1746, by Canaletto
This painting shows the artist in his late 40s, around the time he moved to London, which can be seen in the background.

View of basin of St. Mark's Square, Venice, c.1735, by Canaletto
Canaletto's view shows Venice's Ducal Palace, the campanile, or bell tower, and St. Mark's Square. He captures the architectural detail and the liveliness of the Grand Canal.

realistic as photographs. They became very popular with wealthy foreigners who visited Venice and wanted a souvenir to take home with them. The city was just as famous then as it is now for its beauty and artistic treasures, and it was high on the list of places to visit for foreign tourists.

Many of these tourists were English. At the time, it was the custom for young English gentlemen to spend a year or two traveling around Europe, as a way of completing their general education. This period abroad was known as the "Grand Tour."

For most of his English sales, Canaletto relied on two British agents. The first was Owen McSwiney, who had gone bankrupt in London and had moved to Italy to escape his creditors. He had good contacts, including many aristocratic art collectors.

Canaletto's second and more important agent was Joseph Smith. He had settled in Venice in around 1700 to work as a banker, and remained there for the rest of his life. Smith handled most of Canaletto's work during the 1730s, when the artist was at the height of his popularity. In addition to acting as a contact with potential customers, Smith also bought many of Canaletto's works for his own magnificent art collection.

A MOVE TO ENGLAND

By the 1740s, Canaletto was famous. But his fortune soon changed. In 1741, his business was badly affected by the outbreak of the War of the Austrian Succession, which involved several European countries. The seven-year war made foreign travel difficult, and Canaletto's tourist trade virtually dried up. Since most of his best customers came from England, he decided to move there himself.

At first, Canaletto found plenty of work in England. Several noblemen commissioned him to produce paintings of their country houses. In addition, he painted many superb pictures of the Thames River, one of his favorite subjects. He may have had memories of the bright sunshine back home in Italy, for he painted the normally muddy waters of the Thames a brilliant blue.

Some people, however, felt that Canaletto's style had become mechanical and repetitive, compared with his earlier works. There were even rumors that he was not the real Canaletto at all, but an impostor. Toward the mid-1750s, he was once again short of work.

This led him to return home to Venice in 1756. But he would never enjoy his previous level of success. He was almost 60 by this time, and he produced relatively few paintings in the remaining 12 years of his life.

Although Canaletto was finally elected to the Venice Academy of

MAJOR WORKS	
C.1727	ST. MARK'S SQUARE
C.1728	THE STONEMASON'S YARD
C.1730	THE BUCINTORO RETURNING TO THE MOLO ON ASCENSION DAY
C.1735	BASIN OF ST. MARK'S SQUARE; THE FEAST DAY OF SAINT ROCH
1742	ENTRANCE TO THE GRAND CANAL
1754	OLD WALTON BRIDGE OVER THE THAMES

Painting and Sculpture in 1763, this was a paltry honor compared with the great esteem in which he had been held in England. His fellow Venetians never really appreciated the extent of his talents. They preferred religious, historical, and mythological paintings to his realistic city views.

A FORGOTTEN MASTER

Near the end of his life, the art world all but forgot Canaletto. He was reduced to sketching in public in order to attract work. In 1760, two English tourists saw him sketching in St. Mark's Square, the heart of Venice. He was delighted when they recognized him from the style of his work. On April 19, 1768, Canaletto died, at the age of 70. There were rumors that he had amassed a fortune, but apart from his modest house and 28 paintings in his studio, the only possessions that he left were his bed and some old clothes.

WILLIAM HOGARTH

One of England's most influential artists, William Hogarth achieved fame as both a painter and an engraver. Some of his best-known works vividly captured the realities of life in his native London.

William Hogarth was born in London on November 10, 1697. His family was very poor: His father had been a failed schoolteacher, writer, and coffeehouse owner. By the time William was 12, the whole family was living in the Fleet, a debtors' prison, where they all remained for the next three years.

LEARNING TO ENGRAVE

After their release in 1712, William began a seven-year apprenticeship with an engraver. He left after six years to set up his own engraving business. Engraving is a method of making prints by cutting lines or dots into a hard surface. When the design is reproduced by printing on paper, the picture is called an engraving, or print. Artists like Hogarth would make engravings of existing paintings, as well as inventing original works of art.

By now, his father had died, and William was responsible for the family's welfare. At first, Hogarth concentrated on producing book illustrations and business cards. Then he decided to learn to paint. He attended free classes run by a well-known history painter, Sir James Thornhill. In 1729, Hogarth ran away with Thornhill's daughter, Jane, and the couple got married. They enjoyed a happy marriage.

DRIVING AMBITION

Having learned the techniques of oil painting, Hogarth now turned to producing group portraits, called conversation pieces, for the aristocracy. Although he was an excellent portraitist, his ambitions lay elsewhere. He was not suited to flattering fashionable and wealthy clients. He dismissed the work as mere "face-painting."

Hogarth also disliked the aristocratic obsession with foreign art, which he considered harmful to the careers of English artists. He complained about the

The Painter and his Pug, 1745,
by William Hogarth
Hogarth's self-portrait shows him at the age of 48, his dog by his side.

"shiploads of dead Christs, Madonnas, and Holy Families" that were flooding the London art market at the time. He preferred to paint ordinary people rather than these religious characters.

INSPIRED BY LONDON

Perhaps as a result of his experience of poverty and life in the debtors' prison, Hogarth was always bitterly critical of society's corruption and immorality. In his works, he expressed his distaste for the depravity he saw all around him. The streets of his native London provided Hogarth with plenty of material. The city could be both ugly and

> "I ... admire nature beyond the finest pictures."
> (Hogarth on his source of inspiration)

magnetic. All human life was there. While some people made their fortunes overnight and enjoyed a life of luxury, others lived in squalor, and fell into crime, drunkenness, and prostitution.

HOGARTH'S MORAL TALES

In 1731, Hogarth and his wife moved into her father's house in central London. That year, he painted *A Harlot's Progress*. This was his first narrative series, a sequence of paintings that tells a tale and teaches a moral lesson. The six paintings of the series

HOGARTH'S LINE

Hogarth's curving line of beauty and grace was the basis of his artistic theory. It is evident in all his work.

Hogarth set out his theory of art in "The Analysis of Beauty." He wrote this treatise because he thought the view of an artist was more important than that of a critic or connoisseur.

For Hogarth, the secret of beauty was the "serpentine" or curving line (*right*). This appears in his self-portrait, visible on his palette, like a trademark. It can also be seen in small details, as in the *Marriage Contract* from the *Marriage à la Mode* series. The unwilling bride-to-be curls her handkerchief between her fingers, showing her indifference.

Despite the great activity in Hogarth's paintings, his figures

charted the story of an honest country girl, Moll Hackabout, who meets her downfall in the city.

Hogarth feared that the paintings would not sell very well. So, to boost his income, he had the idea of engraving and selling prints of the series. The prints were enormously popular. A far wider audience could afford to buy prints, which were much cheaper than

are graceful. Curving lines link groups of people, giving them a sense of life and movement. This reflects the artist's idea that his figures are acting in a kind of theater, sending out silent signals to the viewer.

paintings. By 1733, Hogarth had made his reputation, and had set up a shop as a print-seller. This and subsequent narrative series suited him perfectly, and earned him a decent living.

Hogarth felt that his "modern moral subjects," or depictions of contemporary life, were just as worthy of art as historical subjects, or stories from the Bible or mythology. He chose "the book of nature" as his subject matter because he wanted to appeal to ordinary people as well as connoisseurs.

The scenes that Hogarth chose to depict showed an unlovely side of London life. Yet the pictures were always beautifully painted. He believed that his kind of art should be viewed as equal to the highest art of the Italian Renaissance. He even hung a portrait of the Flemish master, Anthony Van Dyck, outside his shop, to show that his own work formed part of this great tradition.

PROTECTING HIS WORK

Hogarth's next series, *A Rake's Progress* of 1734, told the story of Tom Rakewell, who squanders his fortune in riotous living, only to end his life in an asylum. Like *The Harlot's Progress*, it proved to be popular. But Hogarth was soon a victim of his own success. His prints were in such demand that other engravers produced and sold pirated copies. To try to protect his interests and reputation, Hogarth campaigned for an engravers' copyright act, which became law in 1735.

At this time, Hogarth set up his own art school, St. Martin's Academy. He had mixed feelings about art schools, knowing that they could stifle initiative and originality. But he also appreciated the value of some kind of training for aspiring artists. He ran his own school in an informal, democratic way.

CHARITY WORKER

During the 1730s, Hogarth became involved in charities. In 1739, he helped set up the Foundling Hospital for aban-

Marriage à la Mode (1): The Marriage Contract, c.1743, by William Hogarth
This painting is part of a series that savagely attacks the idea of marriage for money. The unwilling bride and groom, symbolized by the chained dogs, ignore each other to the left of the scene, while their fathers draw up a financial contract with a lawyer.

doned children. He arranged for artists to hang their work in the hospital, thus attracting the public to the institution and promoting both the artists and the charity at the same time. His portrait of Captain Thomas Coram, the hospital's founder, is one of his finest.

BITING SATIRE

Hogarth was less successful with his next major series, *Marriage à la Mode*. This was a savage satirical attack on the high-society practice of marrying for money and convenience rather than love. The six paintings tell of an impoverished aristocrat who marries off his son to a wealthy merchant's daughter. The marriage turns into a nightmare of infidelity and ends with the unhappy couple's deaths. The engravings met with less success than Hogarth's earlier works, probably because they attacked the very people who were most likely to buy them.

The disappointment of the series' lukewarm reception was soon followed by another. In 1743, Hogarth auctioned his paintings, hoping to show that they were as popular as imported Italian Old Masters. The sale was a failure. When

> "Other pictures we see, Hogarth's we read."
> (19th-century critic, William Hazlitt)

he tried another auction several years later with the same result, he was so angry that he tore down Van Dyck's portrait from outside his shop.

INCREASING BITTERNESS

Perhaps Hogarth's greatest late work was his final narrative series, *The Election*, which he painted in 1753-54 and then engraved, as before. It reveals, with color and comedy, the corrupt political practices that were rife in the country. Yet although it has Hogarth's customary humor, it is humor with a cutting edge of disillusionment with man's actions in a corrupt society. Hogarth was increasingly bitter and angry with the world as he grew older.

SKILL IN ALL FIELDS

Although he established himself primarily as an engraver, Hogarth also tried his hand at other, more traditional, kinds of art. He practiced portraiture, decorative mural—or wall—painting, religious and historical painting. He was very successful in these fields, but it seemed as if he worked at them only to prove that he could do them.

Hogarth particularly excelled at portraiture. He was equally good at formal images, such as his portrait of the bishop of Winchester, and more intimate, informal portrayals. And he had unrivaled skill in capturing the lively, innocent nature of children.

ACTIVE TO THE END

Hogarth never abandoned his patriotic support of English art. In 1759, he chose an uncharacteristic subject from classical mythology called *Sigismunda*. This was because he was furious that a picture of the same subject had recently been sold in London for a large sum, simply because it was thought to be by a famous Italian artist. Hogarth's own version failed to sell, but he fought to get it engraved right up until his death in 1764.

MAJOR WORKS

c.1731	A HARLOT'S PROGRESS
1734	A RAKE'S PROGRESS
1740	CAPTAIN CORAM
c.1743	MARRIAGE À LA MODE
1747	INDUSTRY AND IDLENESS
1751	BEER STREET; GIN LANE
c.1753-54	THE ELECTION

JOSHUA REYNOLDS

The most versatile portraitist of the 18th century, Reynolds was also an outstanding writer on art. His enormously successful career helped to bring a new status to artists in England.

Joshua Reynolds was born on July 16, 1723, in Plympton Earl's, a small town in the county of Devon, in southwest England. His father, the Reverend Samuel Reynolds, was both a clergyman and headmaster of the local school, so Joshua grew up in a pious and scholarly atmosphere. There were books on art in his father's library, and, from an early age, Joshua's ambition was to be a painter.

STUDYING ART

In 1740, he went to London to study under Thomas Hudson, one of the most successful portraitists in the country. After three years with Hudson, Reynolds set up on his own as a portraitist, working in his native Devon and in London.

From the very beginning of his career, Reynolds believed that painting should be a dignified and learned profession. At this time, successful portrait painters in England could earn a lot of money, but they did not have a high social status. Many people regarded them in the same way that they regarded dressmakers—as skillful craftsmen rather than creative artists. Reynolds wanted to change this.

TO ITALY

Reynolds decided he needed to travel abroad and experience the world. He knew that Italy was the place where the visual arts were most loved and respected, and he wanted to see the unmatched artistic treasures there. His chance came in 1749, when he met a young naval officer, Augustus Keppel, who was about to sail for the Mediterranean. Keppel invited Reynolds to accompany him. It was the start of a lifelong friendship.

Reynolds spent more than two years in Italy, mainly in Rome, supported by money from two of his sisters. He

Self-portrait, 1748, by Joshua Reynolds
This painting shows the artist at the age of 25. Holding his palette and brush, he shades his eyes from the light.

Three Ladies Adorning a Term of Hymen, 1773, by Joshua Reynolds
One of Reynolds's most ambitious works shows the three daughters of Sir William Montgomery at a term—a sculpted figure on a pedestal—of Hymen, the god of marriage.

studied the remains of ancient Roman art and the paintings of the great artists of the Renaissance, particularly Michelangelo and Raphael. Italy can be chilly in winter, and while copying paintings by Raphael in the Vatican, Reynolds caught a severe cold that left him deaf for a short time. He had a hearing disorder for the rest of his life.

Reynolds returned to England in October 1752, at the age of 29. Early the following year, he settled in London, where he would live for the rest of his life. There were other talented portraitists in London at this time, but Reynolds quickly outstripped them, and was soon both busy and prosperous.

The portrait that established his reputation was a magnificent, full-length portrayal of his friend, Augustus Keppel. Reynolds based Keppel's pose on that of a famous ancient statue called the *Apollo Belvedere*, which he had studied in Rome. This kind of "quotation"—using a pose or gesture from the art of the past—was one way in which Reynolds tried to give portraiture a new dignity and seriousness.

Reynolds produced a huge number of portraits, but he rarely repeated himself, for he was remarkably versatile and inventive. He was equally good at painting men, women, or children, responding to the personality of each individual, from tough old soldiers to elegant society ladies, and from dignified statesmen to playful children. His only serious rival as the best portraitist in England was Thomas Gainsborough, who expressed both envy and admiration when he exclaimed of Reynolds: "Damn him! How various he is!"

AN ORGANIZED WORKER

There were other reasons for Reynolds' success apart from his versatility. He was able to put people at ease when he was painting them. And he was very well-organized and hardworking. He recorded his appointments with clients in what he called his "sitter books." These reveal that Reynolds usually had an average of about three clients a day coming to his studio; on exceptionally busy days he sometimes had as many as six. If a customer failed to turn up for the appointment, he painted a friend or called in some little beggar child off the streets to pose.

Even on the day he was knighted in 1769, he did not forget business—he fitted the ceremony at St. James's Palace between a morning and afternoon studio session. He never married. His sister, Frances, was his housekeeper for many years, and in later life, two of his nieces looked after him.

One of the peaks of Reynolds' career came in 1768, when the Royal Academy was founded in London. The aim of the Academy was to raise the prestige of art in Britain. Reynolds's success made him the obvious choice for president, and he occupied the post for the rest of his life.

As part of his duties, he gave a series of annual "discourses," or lectures, to the students. These are beautifully written and full of interesting observations. They were published as a book, which many people regard as the most impressive work on art theory written in English in the 18th century.

Reynolds' eyesight started to fail when he was in his 60s, and he stopped painting in 1789. He died in London on February 23, 1792, and was buried with great ceremony in St. Paul's Cathedral. He was the first English artist ever to be honored in this way.

MAJOR WORKS

1754	COMMODORE KEPPEL
C.1762	NELLY O'BRIEN; GARRICK BETWEEN TRAGEDY AND COMEDY
C.1773	SELF-PORTRAIT IN ACADEMIC ROBES
1773	THREE LADIES ADORNING A TERM OF HYMEN
1781	DEATH OF DIDO
1784	SARAH SIDDONS AS THE TRAGIC MUSE
1787	LORD HEATHFIELD

GEORGE STUBBS

One of the greatest animal painters of all time, Stubbs was particularly famous for his pictures of horses. To understand animals better, he became a student of anatomy. His work unites the worlds of art and science.

George Stubbs was born in Liverpool, northwest England, on August 25, 1724. As a boy, George learned the trade of his father, John, who was a leatherworker. He spent all his spare time drawing, however. When his father died in 1741, he decided to become an artist.

A NATURAL CURIOSITY

The 17-year-old worked briefly with a local artist, but mainly he taught himself. While he was learning about art, Stubbs also began to teach himself anatomy—the way the body works—by dissecting animals, for he had great curiosity about the natural world.

In about 1745, Stubbs moved to York, in the north of England, where he earned his living as a portrait painter. He also studied anatomy at the local hospital. One of the doctors there, John Burton, commissioned the young artist to illustrate a book he was writing on midwifery—the practice of assisting at childbirth. This was published in 1751.

Some of the illustrations were based on Stubbs's own dissection of a woman who had died in childbirth. Stubbs's illustrations were made in the form of etchings—prints in which the design is engraved onto a copper printing plate by means of acid. The resourceful Stubbs taught himself the technique. Although his first attempts were slightly unsophisticated, he soon became a very skillful printmaker.

DISSECTING HORSES

In 1754, Stubbs made a brief visit to Italy to study the art treasures there. After his return to England, he lived in Liverpool for two years, and then, in 1756, he moved to a farmhouse in a remote part of Lincolnshire, east England. He chose this secluded place because he planned to produce a book on the anatomy of horses, and he knew

Portrait of George Stubbs,
by Ozias Humphry
The date of this portrait, by Stubbs's contemporary, Humphry, is unknown.

Mares and Foals in a River Landscape, 1753, by George Stubbs
Stubbs's series of paintings of horses in a lyrical English landscape are some of his most popular works. Stubbs drew brilliantly accurate portraits of his patrons' horses from life.

that neighbors would object to the horrible sight and smell of the rotting horse carcasses he would have to dissect. For 18 months, he worked on his dissections, assisted only by Mary Spencer, his common-law wife. They had two children: George Townley Stubbs, who became an engraver, and Mary, who died young.

A MASTER OF ANATOMY

In 1758, Stubbs moved to London, where he lived for the rest of his life. He hoped that he would be able to find an engraver there to make book illustrations from his anatomical drawings, but eventually he decided to do the work himself. It was a slow process, but his magnificent book, *The Anatomy of the Horse*, was at last published in 1766.

By this time, Stubbs had gained a reputation as an outstanding horse painter. His illustrations were admired for their scientific accuracy as well as for their beauty. This was a good time to be a horse painter, for it was a golden age in English racing. Stubbs painted many "portraits" of champion racehorses, sometimes with their jockeys or proud owners. He also produced hunting scenes and a series of dramatic paintings showing a lion attacking a horse—he is said to have witnessed such an attack in north Africa, when he was returning from Italy.

With his sound knowledge of the animal's physique, Stubbs was able to produce startlingly accurate images of horses. For his portrait of a horse called Whistlejacket, for example, he probed every muscle, tendon, and blood vessel that lay beneath the surface of the skin. The resulting realism even convinced the horse. It is said that one day, as Stubbs was at work outside on the painting, Whistlejacket suddenly caught sight of it. He began "to stare and look wildly at the picture, endeavoring to get at it, to fight and kick it."

EXOTIC CREATURES

In addition to horses, Stubbs painted a variety of other animals. At this time, the British were expanding into Africa, the Americas, and the Far East, stimulating an interest in the wild animals of these places. Stubbs painted the first "African ass"—now known as the zebra—ever seen in England, as well as a moose, a rhinoceros, and other beasts that must have looked very strange to European eyes.

FINANCIAL STRUGGLE

Stubbs had many rich and important patrons. His career was at its peak in the 1760s, but in the 1780s he began to have financial problems. This was not because there was any drop in the quality of his work, but rather because he worked on projects that interested him but did not make money.

Stubbs's inquisitive mind meant that he was fascinated by experimenting with different media and techniques. He collaborated with the famous potter, Josiah Wedgwood, in producing pictures that were painted on large enamel plaques instead of canvas. This project produced interesting results artistically—but financially, it was a disaster.

In the early 1790s, the Prince of Wales—later King George IV—began to commission work from Stubbs. Despite this, Stubbs struggled to survive financially. He had to be rescued from poverty by Isabella Saltonstall, a loyal friend and patron.

CONTINUED ENERGY

Yet his problems did not affect the quality of his work, or his energy. When he died on July 10, 1806, aged 81, the ever enthusiastic and resilient Stubbs was at work on a massive book that might have daunted a man half his age. This was *A Comparative Anatomical Exposition of the Structure of the Human Body with that of a Tiger and a Common Fowl*. The drawings that he made for this book show that Stubbs kept his artistic skill and his spirit of scientific curiosity undimmed to the very end of his long life.

MAJOR WORKS

c.1762	HORSE ATTACKED BY A LION
1762	WHISTLEJACKET
1765	CHEETAH AND STAG WITH TWO INDIANS
1766	THE ANATOMY OF THE HORSE
1770	WHITE HORSE ATTACKED BY A LION
1785	HAYMAKERS
1799	HAMBLETONIAN RUBBING DOWN

JEAN-HONORÉ FRAGONARD

No artist offers us a more colorful view of life in pre-Revolutionary France than Fragonard. He painted his charming and sensual pictures for an aristocratic society that appreciated taste, elegance, and a leisurely attitude to life.

Jean-Honoré Fragonard was born on April 5, 1732, in Grasse, a village in southern France. He seems to have had a carefree childhood, but this did not last long. In 1738, his father, a glove-maker, lost all his money in a failed business venture. The family moved to Paris and, at the age of 15, Fragonard started work in a lawyer's office. Here, he spent so much of his time drawing cartoons, that his parents agreed to let him train as an artist instead.

AN EXCELLENT TRAINING

His first master was Jean-Baptiste Chardin, who specialized in still-life painting. Fragonard found the discipline in Chardin's studio too tough and, after six months, he left. He was far happier working for his next teacher, François Boucher. Boucher was the most popular painter of the time, and the favorite artist of King Louis XV's mistress, Madame de Pompadour. Under Boucher's supervision, Fragonard designed tapestries for distinguished patrons.

Boucher suggested that the youth enter the contest for the Prix de Rome. This award would increase his reputation and give him the chance to study in Italy. Fragonard won the prize in 1752, and went to Rome four years later.

The journey proved a mixed blessing. He did not enjoy the traditional practice of drawing copies of classical statues, and the pictures by famous artists, such as Michelangelo and Raphael, overawed him. The main benefit of Fragonard's Italian trip was his meeting with the Abbé de Saint-Non in 1760. The Abbé, a wealthy collector and amateur artist, encouraged the young man to develop his own style.

Fragonard returned to Paris in 1761 to resume his career. He spent much of the next four years working in private. But in 1765, he achieved public success. His picture of *Coresus sacrificing*

Presumed self-portrait, c.1750, by Jean-Honoré Fragonard
This shows the elegant young Fragonard when he was still a student with Boucher.

The Swing, 1766, by Jean-Honoré Fragonard
Fragonard set his most famous work in an exotic, dreamlike garden, which gave the scene a sense of fantasy. He paid great attention to the woman's frothy pink dress, which billows out and catches the brilliant sunlight, while her shoe flies off toward her hidden lover.

himself to save Callirhoë, a subject taken from Greek history, was well received by the critics, and gained him membership in the French Academy.

The academy was the most important artistic body in France and its approval set the seal on Fragonard's reputation. Together with his success in winning the Prix de Rome, it seemed likely that he would spend the rest of his career painting large pictures of historical or religious subjects.

A NEW DIRECTION

Instead, Fragonard's career went in a totally different direction. In 1766, he was asked to paint *The Swing*. His client, the Baron de Saint-Julien, wanted a picture showing a young woman frolicking on a swing, while her lover watched from the bushes below.

In almost any other age, such a theme might have seemed tasteless or immoral. But the art collectors of Fragonard's time liked buying paintings which treated love as a harmless pastime. *The Swing* proved a vital turning point in Fragonard's career. From this point onward, he received a steady stream of orders for lighthearted amorous pictures of this kind.

It is not hard to see why Fragonard followed this course. The larger, historical paintings might have earned him more money and won the French Academy's approval—but they would not have suited his temperament. He would have needed to labor slowly and carefully over them.

Fragonard far preferred working at speed. Often he only sketched the figures in lightly, with a few deft strokes of the brush. This helped to create the sense of passion and energy that flickers across his paintings. In a portrait of the Abbé de Saint-Non, Fragonard completed the entire picture in just one hour.

Fragonard painted a wide variety of subjects, including landscapes and portraits and pictures of children, but he is best remembered for his scenes of young love. These were very popular among the aristocracy during the leisurely years of the mid-18th century.

DECLINE IN FAVOR

As the French Revolution drew nearer, however, Fragonard's work began to go out of fashion. When the revolution broke out in 1789, Fragonard fled to Grasse. He returned to Paris two years later, but his style of painting had been swept away, along with the society which had supported it. Jacques-Louis David (*see page 52*) helped him obtain an administrative job. But with the rise of Napoleon, Fragonard lost this job, and spent his last years in poverty and neglect. He died on August 22, 1806.

MAJOR WORKS

1765	CORESUS SACRIFICING HIMSELF TO SAVE CALLIRHOË
1766	THE SWING
1770-72	THE PURSUIT OF LOVE
c.1775	THE BOLT
c.1776-78	BLIND MAN'S BUFF

JOHN SINGLETON COPLEY

The outstanding American painter of the 18th century, Copley was brilliantly successful in both his own country and in England. But at the end of his career his popularity waned. He died broken in spirit, and in serious debt.

Richard and Mary Copley emigrated to America from Ireland in around 1735. Their son, John Singleton, was born on July 3, 1738, probably in Boston. Richard, who ran a tobacconist's shop, died when John was very young. Mary remarried in May 1748, when her son was almost ten.

AWARE OF ART

Mary's second husband, Peter Pelham, earned his living partly as an engraver. He had worked in London, and he owned a good collection of engravings of European works of art as well as many books on painting. This meant that from an early age, John was aware of a great world of culture on the far side of the Atlantic.

In February 1749, Mrs Pelham had another child, Henry, but she was widowed again when Peter Pelham died in December 1751. So, at the age of 13, John Copley found himself fatherless for the second time. He decided that he had to work to help support his mother and young half brother. Pelham had left the tools of his trade to the family, and John taught himself how to engrave and paint. He concentrated on portraits, for these were virtually the only type of picture the American colonists wanted.

A SKILLED PORTRAITIST

There were few other talented artists working in Boston at this time, and so Copley rapidly gained clients. While he was still only in his teens, he established himself as the leading artist in his native city. And by his early 20s, he was painting the best portraits that America had ever seen.

The young artist achieved his success by hard work and perseverance, as well as natural talent, learning as he went along. He painted directly on the canvas without preliminary drawings. He often made changes as he struggled

Self-portrait, c.1784,
by John Singleton Copley
The artist painted this portrait after settling in London in the mid-1770s.

for the effect he wanted. The figures in his early pictures are sometimes a little stiff, but virtually from the beginning of his career he had a wonderful skill for conveying character.

A SENSE OF LIFE

One of the ways in which Copley captured a sense of life and vitality was by showing people relaxed, and in their own environment. He avoided formal poses and settings. Many of his portraits capture the sitter with such immediacy that they seem almost to be pausing in the middle of their daily life.

In 1766, Copley was encouraged to travel to England, when a painting of his went on show in London. The work, *Boy with a Squirrel*, was probably the first American painting to be exhibited abroad, and it was much admired by critics. Yet Copley hesitated to leave his native country for good. He was rich and famous there. He would remain in America for eight more years.

A HAPPY MARRIAGE

Throughout the 1760s, Copley had all the work he could handle. He was painting an average of two portraits a month. Many of Copley's clients came from Boston's prosperous merchant class. On November 17, 1768, he married Susanna Farnham Clarke, the daughter of one of the richest men in the city. Susanna—or "Sukey," as her husband called her—was a devoted wife, who took a great interest in Copley's work. The marriage lasted until his death 46 years later, and the couple had six children.

WATSON AND THE SHARK

Copley's lively depiction of a true-life drama was the sensation of the Royal Academy exhibit of 1778.

Copley's most famous painting, *Brook Watson and the Shark*, was inspired by a narrow escape from the savage jaws of death. In 1749, the 14-year-old Brook Watson was swimming in Havana Harbor in Cuba, an island in the West Indies. when he was attacked by a shark (*above right*). His companions in a boat just managed to pull him to safety, but he lost a leg.

Almost 30 years later, when Watson was a successful businessman in London, he commissioned Copley to paint a picture of the incident. Brook Watson later went on to be Lord Mayor of London.

Soon after getting married, Copley bought land on Beacon Hill, a rural area, and had a large house built there. But before he and his wife could move in, he was invited to visit New York City, where, a friend assured him, he would do good business. In 1771, Copley traveled to New York, where he would stay for seven months. His friend was right. There had never been a painter of

Copley certainly conveyed the terror and drama of the event, and his large picture won a great deal of praise. People admired the combination of drama and grandeur of the painting, even comparing it to the works of the great Italian masters. Some critics, however, complained that the shark was not very realistic. There is probably a good reason for this: It is unlikely that Copley had ever seen a shark in real life. All the same, the painting stunned visitors to London's Royal Academy, and made Copley's name.

his skill in the city, and the artist had so much work that, as he wrote to his half brother, "I hardly get time to eat …."

He did find time to visit Philadelphia, however, where he saw a major picture collection. This included copies of Italian Old Master paintings, which impressed him greatly, and inspired him to look further than America. Although still in his early 30s, Copley was the undisputed head of his profession. He knew this—but he also knew that the competition in his own country was modest. He longed to see how he would match up against the best painters in Europe.

TO EUROPE

For years, Copley hesitated to leave America, but eventually he was swayed by politics. For some time, there had been unrest against British rule in America; if this turned to revolution, the artist knew that his business could suffer drastically. This seemed the perfect time to visit Europe, so in June 1774, Copley at last set sail. He intended

> "A genius who bids fair to rival the great masters of the ancient Italian schools."
> (a critic on Copley)

to return to Boston, but in fact he never saw America again. After a visit to Italy to study, he settled in London, where he would spend the remaining 40 years of his life.

Copley was soon busy painting portraits for distinguished clients. Already, however, his mind was turning away from portraiture to another type of picture. Like most of his contemporaries, he believed that the most impor-

Watson and the Shark, 1778, by John Singleton Copley
In this exciting painting, Brook Watson's friends try desperately to rescue him from the jaws of a shark. Havana Harbor can be seen in the background. The men in the boat look panic-stricken, as the boat rocks on the murky green water.

tant branch of art was "history painting," in which grand figures were depicted in some noble setting, usually taken from religion or mythology.

In Rome, he had painted a small picture of *The Ascension of Christ*, to try out his hand in this field. But in London he got the opportunity to test his powers in a much more ambitious and original way. A wealthy merchant called Brook Watson commissioned him to paint a picture depicting a dramatic incident from his youth, when a shark had attacked him in Cuba's Havana Harbor.

AN EXCITING PAINTING

Copley's *Watson and the Shark* was acclaimed as a masterpiece when it was exhibited in 1778 at London's Royal Academy. It was one of the earliest history paintings to show the figures in contemporary dress. Previously, artists depicted the characters in a painting in ancient-looking costume because this was considered more noble and impressive. Copley's work of art was also the first to treat a subject that had been chosen simply because it was exciting. Traditionally, history paintings were meant to have a serious and morally uplifting tale to tell.

> "You can scarcely help discoursing with them, asking questions and receiving answers." (John Adams, second U.S. president, on Copley's portraits)

Copley followed up this success with other paintings depicting exciting contemporary events. These included *The Death of the Earl of Chatham*, showing a famous politician collapsing from a stroke as he rose to speak in the English Parliament, and *The Death of Major Peirson*, a battle scene in which a young British soldier dies leading his men to victory against the French.

The British king, George III, admired *The Death of Major Peirson* so much that he commissioned Copley to paint a portrait of his three daughters. Copley must have hoped that this work, which was exhibited at the Royal Academy in 1785, would set the seal on his career.

Instead, it marked the beginning of the artist's decline. One reviewer referred sarcastically to the "delightful disorder" of the picture. And some people thought that in trying to match the elegance of the best portraits he saw in England, Copley had lost the bold vigor that made his American portraits so memorable.

DECLINE AND DEATH

There was another reason for Copley's decline. The Royal Academy had honored him by awarding him membership in 1779. But Copley showed some of his history paintings privately, annoying other Royal Academy members. Gradually, the American's popularity waned, and after about 1800, he sold little work. His final years were deeply sad, as he grew ill, and lost the "powers of mind."

Copley died peacefully on September 9, 1815, aged 77, after a stroke. He left large debts, which were paid off by his son, John Singleton Copley, Jr.

MAJOR WORKS

1765	THE BOY WITH A SQUIRREL
1768	PAUL REVERE
1777	THE COPLEY FAMILY
1778	BROOK WATSON AND THE SHARK
1779-81	THE DEATH OF THE EARL OF CHATHAM
1783	THE DEATH OF MAJOR PEIRSON

BENJAMIN WEST

The first American painter to achieve success in Europe, West was an influential figure on both sides of the Atlantic. The freshness of his ideas caused a revolution in the way artists depicted great scenes from modern history.

Benjamin West was born on October 10, 1738, near Philadelphia in Pennsylvania, into a Quaker family of ten children. His father was an innkeeper. Benjamin is said to have loved drawing from an early age, and he painted his first surviving pictures in about 1752, when he was only 14.

MAKING HIS MARK

By the mid-1750s, he was earning a reputation throughout Pennsylvania as a portrait painter. At this stage, his work was sometimes naive and awkward, mainly because there were few accomplished local artists from whom he could learn. After the arrival of an English artist, John Wollaston, in the late 1750s, however, West's portraits grew more sophisticated.

In about 1756, West painted his first historical subject, *The Death of Socrates*. It was a remarkable achievement for such a young artist. The choice of subject was very unusual, for almost all the pictures painted in the American colonies up to this time were portraits.

West was obviously a boy of exceptional promise, and influential people began to take an interest in him. One of these was the Reverend William Smith, who invited West to Philadelphia to study ancient history and literature with him. West spent three years there, and then a year in New York City painting portraits, before embarking for Europe in 1760. He knew that if he wanted to fulfill his potential as an artist, he had to see the great art of other countries.

THE NEOCLASSICAL STYLE

West spent three years in Italy, visiting Florence, Rome, and other important art centers. He attracted attention because an American painter was a great novelty. Good-looking and charming, he met many influential people. At

Benjamin West, by George Henry Harlow
This undated portrait probably shows West in his 60s, when he was at the height of his career.

this time, a new artistic style was developing in Italy. It was called Neo-classicism—"new classicism"—because it tried to revive the grandeur and nobility of the art of ancient Rome. West quickly realized that he wanted to work in this style.

ARRIVAL IN ENGLAND

In 1763, West left Italy and went to England. He intended to visit England only briefly on his way back to America, but he was such a success that he stayed there. He would live in London for the rest of his life. His fiancée, Elizabeth Shewell, traveled from Philadelphia to be with him, and they were married in London on September 2, 1764. They had two sons, Raphael—named for the Italian Renaissance painter—and Benjamin junior.

West soon attracted attention and reward for both his portraits and his historical scenes. In 1768, he was one of the founding members of the Royal Academy—a great honor. In the same year, he was introduced to King George III, who admired his work so much that he commissioned West to paint a scene from ancient history, *The Final Departure of Regulus from Rome*. This picture was shown to great acclaim at the Royal Academy's first exhibit in 1769.

HISTORY PAINTING

At this time, "history painting"—which included scenes from religion and mythology—was generally regarded as the most important type of painting. It was considered the most difficult, because it usually involved lots of

AMERICANS IN LONDON

Despite his great prestige and success, West took the time to help his fellow American painters.

In the 18th century, American artists were virtually unknown in Europe. As the first to become an international success, West was an inspiration to many of his countrymen. He was generous with practical help and artistic advice to American artists who came to London (*above right*). Several stayed temporarily in his house in the center of the city.

The first American artist West encouraged was John Singleton Copley. In 1766, Copley sent a picture for exhibit in London. When West saw it, he was so impressed that he wrote to Copley in America to praise his work. He supported the younger

figures arranged in complex groups. It was also considered the most noble branch of art, because it was concerned with great people, events, or ideas.

To make the figures in such paintings look as dignified as possible, painters traditionally depicted them either nude or in ancient-looking costume. This meant that they appeared "timeless," and raised above the everyday world.

artist when he settled in London ten years later.

Among the other American artists whom West helped were Washington Allston, who was also a notable writer; Samuel Morse, who eventually gave up art for science and invented the Morse Code; and Charles Robert Leslie, who became a friend of the English landscape painter, John Constable, and wrote a biography of him.

West, however, decided to change this. In 1770, he produced a picture that revolutionized history painting.

The Death of General Wolfe shows the final moments of the British commander in the battle that secured Canada for the British in 1759. West decided to show Wolfe and the other figures in the kind of uniforms they actually wore at the time, rather than in

ancient costumes. He wanted to apply to contemporary history the same concern for accuracy that was traditionally applied to classical subjects. The president of the Royal Academy, Sir Joshua Reynolds (*see page 22*), advised West against this, and even the king said he thought it was "very ridiculous to exhibit heroes in coats, breeches, and cocked hats."

But the artist persevered. Although he was not the first painter to try this kind of modern dress history painting, he was the first to produce a picture of this type that was judged such a success. *The Death of General Wolfe* had great dignity and drama. It was so

> "I foresee that this picture will ... occasion a revolution in the art."
> (Joshua Reynolds on West's *The Death of General Wolfe*)

admired when it was exhibited at the Royal Academy that West had to make several copies of it—and both Reynolds and the king had to admit that they had been wrong.

West was no longer concerned with absolute accuracy in his work. While he painted the uniforms faithfully, he used considerable imagination elsewhere. He included portraits of people who

The Death of Nelson, 1806, by Benjamin West
The painting shows Admiral Nelson as he lies dying on board his flagship, the *Victory*, during the Battle of Trafalgar against the French in 1805. He is cradled in the position usually occupied by Christ—18th-century viewers would have recognized the pose at once.

were not actually present at Wolfe's death, but who added to the emotion or prestige of the scene. He also portrayed Wolfe as an idealized hero, not as the alcoholic and bad military leader he was rumored to have been.

The Death of General Wolfe was an enormous financial success as well as an artistic one. When it was shown, thousands of people paid an entry fee to see it. An engraving of the picture was in such demand that, by 1790, West claimed to have made a huge profit from the sales of the print alone. Finally, the example of *General Wolfe*

led to artistic changes, as other artists experimented with modern history paintings. It also led to a rise in exhibit admission fees and in the production of engravings.

A LASTING INFLUENCE

West's public success was clear, and in 1772, he was appointed historical painter to the king. He was virtually the only painter working in England who could make a living from history painting, since the demand was mainly for portraits. In 1775, however, another American painter, John Singleton

Copley (*see page 34*), settled in London. He too showed that an artist with imagination and skill could produce modern history paintings that would appeal to the British public. West had set a magnificent example to follow.

The late 1770s, when the Revolutionary War in America broke out, were a difficult time for West. He was suspected of having sympathy with the rebels against British rule, although he was careful not to express any views on the war openly. For a time, he fell from royal favor, but his career was soon flourishing again. In 1792, he rose to the very top of the artistic profession in England. When Sir Joshua Reynolds died, West succeeded him as president of the Royal Academy.

West disliked public speaking, and some of the other members of the Royal Academy thought he made a poor president. He resigned in 1805, but was asked to return shortly afterward. He took up the post again the following year. He then remained president until his death, serving a total of 27 years.

THE DEATH OF A HERO

West returned to contemporary history when he painted *The Death of Nelson* in 1806. Nelson, the great British naval leader, had admired West's *General Wolfe*. The artist had promised him that he would paint Nelson's own death in a similar style. West produced a monumental vision that had little to do with reality. He justified his lack of accuracy: "There is no other way of representing the death of a Hero but by an Epic representation of it. It must

exhibit the event in a way to excite awe and veneration…. No boy would be animated by a representation of Nelson dying like an ordinary man; his feelings must be roused and his mind inflamed by a scene great and extraordinary."

After 1800, West reworked many of his previous paintings. He still produced exciting new work, however, surprising his critics by painting a series of religious works which earned him the greatest public success of his whole career.

A GREAT REPUTATION

West died in London on March 11, 1820, aged 81, and was buried with great ceremony in St. Paul's Cathedral. The artist's reputation declined after his death, but his place in art history is secure. It was Benjamin West who first made people in Europe take American art seriously, and for this reason he is sometimes referred to as the father of American painting.

MAJOR WORKS

c.1756	THE DEATH OF SOCRATES
1770	THE DEATH OF GENERAL WOLFE
c.1776	SELF-PORTRAIT
1777	SAUL & WITCH OF ENDOR
1786	THE CONVERSION OF ST. PAUL
1806	THE DEATH OF NELSON
1817	DEATH ON A PALE HORSE

ANGELICA KAUFFMANN

One of the most successful women artists of the 18th century, Kauffmann was ambitious and strong-willed. Although self-taught, she triumphed in an art world dominated by men, and became a celebrated artist.

Angelica Kauffmann was born in the Swiss town of Chur on October 30, 1741. Her father, Joseph, was a portraitist who also painted murals, or wall paintings, in churches. From a very young age, Angelica helped him.

Joseph Kauffmann soon realized that his daughter was exceptionally talented. Angelica's skill must have impressed others too, for by the time she was in her teens she was receiving her own commissions. Among the powerful and influential people who asked her to paint their portraits was the duchess of Modena, northern Italy.

AN AMBITIOUS ARTIST

In spite of such encouragement, Angelica was not satisfied. She wanted to try the most difficult and most admired kind of painting: history painting. History painters depicted scenes from ancient history, myths, legends, and the Bible. It was difficult for female artists to get involved in this kind of painting, because they were not allowed to sketch nude figures. Drawing from the nude, which was thought to be essential for an aspiring history painter, was not considered a respectable activity for young ladies. So instead, Angelica copied from books and other paintings.

TRAVELS IN EUROPE

After her mother died in 1757, she traveled around Europe with her father, meeting many different artists, and seeing their work. By her early 20s, Angelica could speak several languages, and was at home in high society.

In June 1762, the father and daughter arrived in Florence, Italy. Here she met Benjamin West (*see page 40*), a young American who was trying to recreate the spirit of classical art in his own painting. This style of art, known as neoclassical, drew its inspiration from

Self-portrait, 1794, by Angelica Kauffmann **Kauffmann shows herself here as a young woman, even though she was really in her early 50s at the time.**

ancient Greek and Roman art, particularly classical sculpture. In the Italian capital, Rome, she came into contact with other leading figures of the neoclassical movement, such as the English artist, Nathaniel Dance, and the Italian, Pompeo Batoni.

At the same time, she had a good business painting portraits of wealthy visitors to Rome. This venture proved so successful that Kauffmann's father decided to give up his own career and become her manager.

A NEW STYLE

Around 1764, Kauffmann produced one of her earliest history paintings, *Penelope at her Loom*. Penelope was a character from the *Odyssey*, a famous ancient poem by the Greek poet, Homer. She was a loyal wife, who stayed faithful to her husband, Odysseus, while he was away at war for more than 20 years. She tricked her many suitors by promising to choose a new husband when she had finished a piece of weaving on her loom. But she never finished the piece, for every night she would unpick the day's work. Angelica may have admired Penelope's determined spirit, for she painted several pictures of the heroine.

ARRIVAL IN ENGLAND

Kauffmann's talent and growing reputation were publicly recognized when, in June 1765, she was elected to St. Luke's Academy, Rome's artists' association. This was a great honor. Shortly afterward, Kauffmann was invited to England by Lady Wentworth, the wife of an English diplomat.

SECRETS OF SUCCESS

Kauffmann was unusual in achieving success at a time when there were few professional women artists.

Kauffmann was the only woman in her century to succeed at history painting. She sold more of this type of art than many male artists, especially in England. Several factors—apart from her talent, and her determination to train herself—help explain why she succeeded where others failed.

Kauffmann may have done better than male artists through her choice of subject matter. She avoided subjects that were dull or distasteful, seeking out instead stories where the emphasis was on relationships, such as *Hector taking leave of Andromache* (above right).

The visit, which began in 1766, was to last 15 years. In London, Kauffmann found herself involved in an artistic circle that included some old friends—Benjamin West and Nathaniel Dance—and some new ones, such as Joshua Reynolds (*see page 22*). Reynolds was busy encouraging neoclassical art, and what he called the "grand manner" of painting in Britain, and he admired

This work shows the touching scene from ancient history when Hector, the leader of the Trojans, leaves his wife, Andromache, to go and fight in a war against the Greeks. The story was one of intense emotion, and Kauffmann painted it more than once. Such subjects, combined with warm colors, helped her paintings become very popular.

Kauffmann also popularized her work through prints. This made it well-known to a wider audience, and available at a reasonable price.

Kauffmann's style very much. The two artists became good friends, and Kauffmann painted an affectionate portrait of Reynolds in 1767.

Her career in England got off to a flying start, perhaps thanks to her novel position as a successful female artist. People found her intelligent and charming, and she seems to have won the hearts of many important people.

Life was not always straightforward, however. In 1767, she was tricked into marrying a notorious con man who claimed to be a Swedish count. When he turned out to be a swindler, the marriage was hastily annulled.

The episode, although embarrassing, may have actually helped her career. Being single meant that she escaped the fate of other female artists, whose ambitions were often frustrated by the demands of marriage and motherhood. Kauffmann remarried in 1781, but, by then, she was already a famous artist with a flourishing career.

JOINING THE ACADEMY

When Britain's first art institute—the Royal Academy—was set up in 1768 with Reynolds as president, Kauffmann was chosen as one of the first members—one of only two women to be honored in this way. At the academy's first exhibit, Kauffmann's history paintings stood out among the other works, most of which were portraits. The artist, James Northcote, wrote that Kauffmann's *Interview of Hector and Andromache*, and *Venus showing Aeneas and Achates the Way to Carthage*, both of 1767, were two "pictures which chiefly attracted the attention of the connoisseurs."

INTERIOR DESIGN

All the same, history paintings were not very fashionable among the English aristocracy. Kauffmann, therefore, continued to paint portraits. This work was well-paid. She also took part in an interior design project for the Royal

Penelope at her Loom, c.1764, by Angelica Kauffmann
This painting shows the loyal Penelope waiting for her husband, Odysseus, to return from war. The dog mirrors his mistress's wistful pose.

Academy, painting four ovals for the council chamber ceiling. These showed the four aspects of painting: *Invention, Composition, Design, and Color*. During her life, Kauffmann's designs appeared on furniture and china.

RETURN TO ITALY

By 1781, Kauffmann was ready to return to Italy. She longed to escape the endless demand for portraits. Also, she had married an Italian artist, Antonio Zucchi, giving her another reason to return to Italy. But she had become so much a part of London life that many people were sad to lose her. One poet wrote her a poem— "Epistle to Angelica Kauffmann"—to express these feelings of loss at her departure.

Back in Rome, her clients included European aristocrats and leaders, such as Prince Youssoupoff of Russia and Emperor Joseph II of Austria. After her father's death in 1782, her husband took over as her manager, and she enjoyed her most productive years.

She and Zucchi traveled to Naples, where Kauffmann was offered the position of royal painter to the king and queen. She turned this great honor down, however. After this, the couple settled in Rome. She kept in touch with the English art circles, and most years sent back works to exhibit at the Royal Academy's annual show.

THE FINAL YEARS

Reflecting on her life, in 1791 she painted *Self-portrait Hesitating between Painting and Music*. This shows her as a young girl, deciding on a painting career, which is seen as the tougher choice. Her own career had had ample rewards, however. She had succeeded at the highest form of art, and her talents had made her a very rich and famous woman.

SLOWING DOWN

Toward the end of her life, she produced less and less work. This may have been because of external events. Her husband died in 1795. The effects of the French Revolution and subsequent military campaigns also made communications and travel difficult. This meant that many potential clients decided against traveling to Italy.

But Kauffmann's fame remained undimmed. She was a leading figure in the cultivated society of Rome and when artists and intellectuals visited Italy, they sought Kauffmann's company. When she died in Rome on November 5, 1807, she was honored with a grand public funeral.

MAJOR WORKS

c.1764	PENELOPE AT HER LOOM
1764	CORIOLANUS ENTREATED BY HIS MOTHER AND HIS WIFE
1767	SIR JOSHUA REYNOLDS; INTERVIEW OF HECTOR AND ANDROMACHE; VENUS SHOWING AENEAS AND ACHATES THE WAY TO CARTHAGE
1791	SELF-PORTRAIT HESITATING BETWEEN PAINTING AND MUSIC

JACQUES-LOUIS DAVID

Few artists have captured the spirit of their age more successfully than David. He was on close terms with the political figures during and after the French Revolution, helping shape the course of events with his art.

Jacques-Louis David was born in Paris on August 30, 1748. His father, a dealer in iron and hardware, lost his life in a duel in 1757. After the tragedy, David was brought up by two uncles, both of whom were architects.

At first, it seemed that he would follow this profession but, by 1765, he had chosen to train as a painter instead. Initially, he studied under François Boucher, a distant cousin of his, who was also the official painter to King Louis XV. But after only a year, he had changed masters, to become a pupil of Joseph-Marie Vien.

A CHANGE IN STYLE

This switch was crucial. Boucher was the leading painter in the light and elegant Rococo style, which was then extremely fashionable. Vien was a less talented artist, but he was in touch with newer artistic developments. He was able to school David in neoclassical theories, which were rapidly becoming more popular among artistic circles.

The neoclassical, or "new classical," style encouraged artists to seek inspiration in the classical art of ancient Greece and Rome. The main qualities of Neoclassicism were dignity, nobility, and heroism. David was skeptical at first but in 1771, urged on by Vien, he entered a competition called the Prix de Rome, which was organized by the French Academy. The winner of this important award would travel to Italy, to study its art in greater detail. David was very confident that he would win the prize. But he was unsuccessful.

After a second failure the following year, David tried to commit suicide. He eventually won the contest at the fourth attempt—he fainted when he heard the news. The three failures had seriously dented his confidence, and sowed the seeds of a lasting resentment toward the artistic establishment.

Self-portrait, 1794,
by Jacques-Louis David
David painted this during his time in prison. He was imprisoned for his political beliefs.

In 1775, he made the journey south to Italy. It was an ideal time to make such a trip. In addition to the classical ruins in Rome itself, David was able to see the remains of the ancient cities of Pompeii and Herculaneum, which had only recently been discovered by archaeologists. The young artist was very impressed by these sights, and made conscious efforts to fill his paintings with the grandeur of the ancient world.

David returned to France in 1780, and swiftly established himself as the leader of the country's neoclassical school of artists. This meant that he based the style of his paintings on Roman statues and drew his subjects from ancient history. More importantly, he adopted the values of classical writers. Honor, duty, and self-sacrifice became major themes in his work. His severe, noble pictures soon won enthusiastic acclaim. With growing success came domestic bliss. In 1782, David married Charlotte Pécoul.

AN AGE OF REVOLUTION

France was now entering a period of social upheaval. The aristocracy, condemned as immoral, became increasingly unpopular among the country's other classes. Many politicians and philosophers looked back to republican Rome as a model state based on order and justice. For such people, David's stern, plain style and serious themes contrasted favorably with the triviality of Rococo art.

David's success reached its peak in 1785, when he showed *The Oath of the Horatii* at the Salon, the official state

THE FRENCH REVOLUTION

David was closely involved with the violent struggle for power during the bloody years of the Revolution.

The French Revolution came about because of widespread dissatisfaction with King Louis XVI and his policies. In June 1789, rebels set up a National Assembly, in defiance of royal authority and, a month later, an angry mob stormed the Bastille, a much-hated state prison. Eventually, the revolutionaries took the king himself captive, and later executed both him and his queen, Marie-Antoinette, on the guillotine (*above right*).

A republic was established, headed by the National Convention—the parliament of the people—to rule in place of the monarchy. This did not bring an

exhibit in the Louvre Palace in Paris. The reaction to the huge painting was enormously enthusiastic. Critics described the work as the "most beautiful picture of the century." It showed the Horatii, three brothers of ancient Rome, swearing to die for their country. Such patriotism and self-sacrifice captured the spirit in France in the years leading up to the Revolution.

end to the violence, however, for the revolutionary leaders argued among themselves as they struggled for power. Many of them also met their death at the guillotine.

Jacques-Louis David was an active member of the new republic's government. He served on a number of revolutionary committees and briefly held the post of president of the National Convention. His enthusiasm for the Revolution placed him in great danger, however, and he was lucky to escape with his life when his close political ally, Robespierre, lost power and was executed in July 1794.

Not long afterward, David chose an even more extreme subject based on the values of ancient Rome—the story of Brutus, a Roman leader who condemned his own sons to death for the sake of his country. The picture was shown at the Salon of 1789, shortly after the storming of the Bastille prison on July 14, 1789, which marked the start of the French Revolution.

The picture of the grieving father caught the republican mood so perfectly that David's pupils had to guard it from attack by supporters of the king. The painting's theme of personal sacrifice and loyalty to the state had

> "No longer will we have to search in ancient history for subjects to exercise our brushes."
> (David, on painting the French Revolution)

taken on a contemporary meaning overnight. Soon, many Frenchmen would be making the sacrifices that David's paintings demanded.

ARDENT REVOLUTIONARY

It is not clear whether the artist intended his pictures to cause such a stir but, once the Revolution broke out, there was no question where his loyalties lay. He joined the National Convention—the revolutionary parliament—sided with rebels such as Robespierre and Marat, two of the leading extreme revolutionaries, and voted for the execution of the king in 1793.

Modern heroes now replaced the warriors of ancient Greece and Rome in his art. Thus, when Marat was murdered in his bathtub, David accepted a request from the Convention to paint a

The Oath of the Horatii, 1785, by Jacques-Louis David
David's early masterpiece secured his reputation as the leading young artist in France. It shows the three Horatii brothers swearing an oath to their father to fight to the end for their native Rome, while the women of the family mourn their inevitable deaths.

picture immortalizing him as a martyr of the Revolution.

After the Revolution, David virtually became the new French republic's artistic dictator. He not only painted its leaders, but shaped its image, designing festivals and ceremonies intended to spread revolutionary ideas. He controlled almost every aspect of artistic life, from what was taught in art schools to what was shown in museums.

Perhaps remembering his early failures to win the Prix de Rome,

David also successfully campaigned for closing the French Academy. He argued that not only did its teaching methods fail to encourage the development of new and exciting young artists, but also that its snobbish system was opposed to the republic's ideals of democracy and equality.

The artist made personal sacrifices for his political beliefs. His wife, a supporter of the king, divorced him in 1794 and, after the fall of Robespierre, David was arrested and thrown into prison. For a time, it seemed that he might end up on the guillotine, a machine with a heavy blade used for beheading. His wife pleaded for mercy, however, and he was released after six months. The couple remarried in 1796.

This narrow escape did not stop him from entering politics again. When Napoleon seized power in 1799, David declared "Bonaparte is my hero!" Napoleon was not so enthusiastic, preferring the work of Antoine-Jean Gros, one of David's pupils. Even so, he recognized the value of an artist of David's quality, and made him his official painter.

THE EMPEROR'S IMAGE

In an age before photography, paintings offered political leaders an ideal way of presenting a certain image to the public. Napoleon hoped that David's art would glamorize his heroism, the success of his military campaigns, and the splendor of his court.

He was not disappointed. David produced a number of pictures glorifying Napoleon's rule. One of the most striking of these was a portrait which showed Bonaparte crossing the Alps on his way to do battle. Napoleon had made the journey on a mule, but he instructed the artist to show him sitting majestically on a horse. David brilliantly achieved a dignified and powerful portrayal of the leader.

David continued to work for Napoleon until 1815, when the emperor was defeated at the Battle of Waterloo by the British, and ousted from power. Once again, this change in political fortunes caused serious problems for the artist.

Some years earlier, he had stated that he would become an enemy of the state if Bonaparte was ever removed. When the monarchy was restored in 1816, David had to go into exile from France.

A FALL IN FAVOR

David settled in Belgium, where he lived for the rest of his life. There he remained true to his principles, refusing to work for Napoleon's enemies, and urging his pupils to paint subjects from ancient history. But by now, his neoclassical style had become outdated, overtaken by the growing Romantic movement—a movement that celebrated qualities such as passion and wildness. Soon, he was virtually forgotten.

In February 1824, David was knocked down by a horse-drawn cab on his way back from the theater. He never recovered, and he died on December 29, 1825. The French authorities refused to allow his body back into the country, so he was buried in Brussels.

MAJOR WORKS

1785	THE OATH OF THE HORATII
1789	BRUTUS RECEIVING THE BODIES OF HIS SONS
1793	MARAT'S LAST BREATH
1794-99	INTERVENTION OF THE SABINE WOMEN
1800	MADAME RÉCAMIER
1805-08	THE CORONATION OF NAPOLEON AND EMPRESS JOSEPHINE

DANIEL DEFOE

Daniel Defoe's life was full of excitement, daring, and adventure. This inspired him to create *Robinson Crusoe*, an imaginative shipwreck story that has been loved by generations of readers.

Defoe's life began in London in 1660 or 1661. His father was a butcher and candlemaker, and Daniel was the youngest of his three children.

Religion played a vital part in Defoe's education because his father was a nonconformist. This means that he disagreed with the established church of the time, and refused to attend services. Daniel was educated by members of the nonconformist church. His education included studying science, which was unusual at the time.

CHOOSING A CAREER

Defoe was a bright boy, but he could not enter either of the country's main universities, Oxford or Cambridge, because of his family's unconventional religious beliefs. His father had hoped that Daniel would become a nonconformist minister; instead his son followed his own path.

During his life he would be a traveler, historian, merchant, and secret agent. He would be kidnapped by pirates and thrown into prison, and would write almost 600 pieces of work. Apart from novels and pamphlets, these included poetry, newspaper articles, biographies, and tales of sea voyages.

DEFOE THE MERCHANT

By his early 20s, Defoe was a highly successful merchant, dealing in all kinds of goods. Spain, Portugal, and the American colonies were especially profitable customers. Trading involved travel, and it was while he was on a trip to Holland that Defoe was taken prisoner by Algerian pirates. He was released when a ransom was paid.

In 1684, Defoe married Mary Tuffley. Her father was a wealthy man, involved in the wine trade, and so Defoe's fortune grew larger. Their wedding, a lavish affair, was the beginning of 47 happy years together.

Defoe in the Pillory, by Eyre Crowe
Defoe was put in the pillory in 1703. Due to the courage of his writing, the crowd, instead of pelting him with filth, cheered him.

In 1685, the duke of Monmouth raised troops and tried to defeat the ruling Catholic king, James II. Defoe, with his Protestant nonconformist beliefs, joined the rebel army at the Battle of Sedgemoor. The king was victorious, and promptly executed Monmouth and many of the rebels.

Defoe fled into hiding—no one knows exactly where. From this secret place, he sent out a series of pamphlets attacking King James.

BACK IN FAVOR

His luck changed in 1689, when William of Orange, a Dutch Protestant, became king of England after the defeated James had fled. Defoe was now back in favor with royalty, and wrote another series of pamphlets—this time praising the new king.

In the meantime, Defoe's business life was not going well. A large number of ships that he had insured had been lost in battle and, in 1692, Defoe was declared bankrupt. Owing thousands of pounds, he was thrown into Newgate debtors' prison. After just one week, however, he managed to talk his way into an agreement with his creditors, and left Newgate. He would never manage to clear his debts completely.

IN TROUBLE AGAIN

Political problems soon surfaced again. King William died in 1702, and there was bitter argument over who should succeed him. Defoe was once again wanted by the authorities, over a pamphlet he had written that criticized the Church. More than once he found

A SAILOR'S LIFE

One of fiction's great survivors, Robinson Crusoe is the hero of a timeless and exciting tale.

Like many of Defoe's stories, *Robinson Crusoe* is a work of fiction written as one person's factual account of events. Defoe probably chose this approach because it was more acceptable to the public, who at this time were much more used to reading nonfiction than fiction.

The hero of the tale is a slave trader on the high seas. He is shipwrecked on a remote desert island and has to learn to survive. After many years, cannibals visit the island. Crusoe saves one of them just before the others are about to eat him. The savage—whom Crusoe names Friday—becomes the

himself jumping out of windows to escape arrest.

In the end, Defoe was arrested, and his pamphlet burned in public by the hangman. He was lucky to escape with his life. He received a fine and an order to stop publishing his opinions for seven years. He was also put in the pillory—clamped into a wooden frame so that the public could throw rubbish

hero's devoted servant (*above*). Friday is good at surviving on the island. But Crusoe teaches Friday English, and eventually takes him back to Europe.

No one had written like this before. This was a believable, exciting story set in the real world. And its hero was a man who endures his situation with strength and dignity.

at him. But an astonishing thing happened when the public saw Defoe in the pillory. Instead of hurling abuse at him, they cheered him, because he had just published an amusing poem on the subject of being pilloried. The authorities sentenced him to three more months in Newgate.

But things soon turned yet again for Defoe. The new monarch, Queen Anne, pardoned Defoe, and gave him a paid post writing positive propaganda about the government. In 1704, he also became a secret agent, working to keep the government in power.

FACT AND FICTION

Defoe's classic novel, *Robinson Crusoe*, was published in 1719. The following year saw the publication of his *Memoirs of a Cavalier*, the first English historical novel ever written.

The plague swept across Europe in 1721, and in 1722, Defoe wrote *A Journal of the Plague Year*, about the previous outbreak of plague that had occurred in 1665. He wrote *Moll Flanders* in the same year. This was a truly modern work: a highly independent and scandalous woman telling her story.

Creating such original characters brought Defoe success and money—but not enough to pay off his debts. His eventful life ended on April 24, 1731.

MAJOR WORKS

1700	TRUE-BORN ENGLISHMAN
1719	ROBINSON CRUSOE
1720	MEMOIRS OF A CAVALIER
1722	A JOURNAL OF THE PLAGUE YEAR; MOLL FLANDERS
1724	ROXANA
1724-26	A TOUR THROUGH THE WHOLE ISLAND OF GREAT BRITAIN

JONATHAN SWIFT

This highly moral clergyman and writer created one of the most memorable stories in English literature—*Gulliver's Travels*. He used the power of his pen to highlight aspects of society in a sharp and entertaining way.

Swift's start in life was not easy. He was born in Dublin, Ireland, in 1667. Both his parents were English, and his father worked as a steward in a law firm. When Swift's father died, just before his birth, his mother was left to bring up two children on barely any money. Baby Jonathan's nurse then ran away to England with him, and his mother spent three years searching for him before they were reunited.

A BRIGHT CHILD

It seems that the boy was reading well by the age of three. At six, he was sent to Kilkenny College in the south of Ireland, where he received an excellent education. Although he was very advanced intellectually, Swift was a moody child, probably because he had such an insecure family background.

Swift's family could not afford to send him to Oxford University in England, and so the bright 14-year-old took his degree at Trinity College, Dublin. He was a typical high-spirited student, missing lectures, getting into trouble. He only received his degree by special arrangement, in 1686.

Three years later, the 22-year-old began work as secretary to a relative, Sir William Temple, at his attractive house in the green, southern English county of Surrey. Temple, a retired diplomat, treated Swift like a son, and encouraged his interest in politics and literature. Swift's hours were very short. This meant that he had enough time to read everything he could get hold of, and also to study for a master's degree—which he needed in order to become a church minister.

While he was working for Sir William, Swift met an eight-year-old girl called Esther Johnson. The two would remain friends for life. This was also the time when he first started suffering from nausea, giddiness, and deafness—

Jonathan Swift, by Charles Jervas
Jervas, an Irish painter who became official portraitist to King George II of England, shows Swift wearing his minister's robes.

the early signs of Ménière's disease, a serious ear ailment from which Swift was to suffer all his life.

A COMPLEX CHARACTER

Swift was a character of contradictions. He loved women but never married, and hated indulgence but was extravagant with food and drink. He was also snobbish yet extremely generous, giving around one-third of his money to the poor. Swift wrote many entertaining letters to Esther, which show a side of his personality that was gossipy and spontaneous.

The writer found the quiet life in Surrey dull, and after five years there, he finally decided to become a minister. Sir William tried his best to persuade Swift to stay, but the young man was determined. He became a minister in 1695. His first post was in Kilroot, near Belfast. Later, he moved to Laracor, close to Dublin.

DIFFICULT REPUTATION

For the next 40 years or so, all kinds of writing poured endlessly from his pen— poems, pamphlets, and satirical tales— stories which hold up human vices and follies to ridicule or scorn. Swift was constantly brimming over with ideas. Although he was a serious and moral man, he was always full of puns, riddles, and witty conversation.

The minister was especially skilled at writing in a sharp, satirical way. He made no attempt to stop himself from making sarcastic comments about the established Church, and this held back his religious career. In 1704, he

GULLIVER'S TRAVELS

In his best-known work, Swift created a character who learned a great deal from his exciting travels.

Gulliver, the hero of Swift's most famous book, is a man who travels far and wide, and has all kinds of bizarre adventures. In the first part of the book, he finds himself shipwrecked on the island Lilliput, which is filled with tiny people (*above right*). In another part of the book, Gulliver arrives in the land of Houyhn-hnms, where horses are morally superior to humans. Eventually, Gulliver grows to hate humans, and can only bear to be in the company of the horses.

The account of Gulliver's travels is not only an exciting adventure. It is also an allegorical tale—a story that has another

published *A Tale of a Tub*. It contained witty, controversial writing about different Christian beliefs. The work was an instant success.

SWIFT THE WRITER

Swift was full of imagination, but he was also very disciplined about his writing, and could put his brilliant thoughts across clearly and forcefully.

meaning—of a man's growing understanding of his own personality. As he goes about his travels, Gulliver learns more and more about himself and humanity in general.

Swift uses the situations that his character meets to make biting satirical comments on the political and social corruption of 18th-century life, especially the poor treatment of the Irish at the hands of the English.

Other great writers, such as the poet Alexander Pope, recognized his genius and became his friend.

Political matters were vitally important to Swift. He was a passionate believer in liberal ideas, such as making monarchy less powerful, and giving more authority to parliaments. In 1707, Swift acted as the representative of the Irish Church in dealings with the English authorities. He went on to become the government's main political writer in Ireland.

Swift had hoped that his political services would make him a bishop, and he was bitterly disappointed when this did not happen. Instead, he was made dean, or head clergyman, of St. Patrick's Cathedral, Dublin, in 1713. He worked hard to make the best of this position. He proposed a range of solutions for the poverty he saw around him. Once, he jokingly suggested that eating children would solve the problem.

Swift's best-loved book, *Gulliver's Travels*, was published in 1726. It appeared under a pen name, as Swift was worried that this satire of modern corruption would provoke a strong public reaction. The book was an immediate success, however.

His friend from Surrey, Esther, died in 1728. For the next 20 years, Swift worked furiously, completing some of his most brilliant writing. In 1745, he suffered a stroke, and died in October. He was buried close to Esther's resting place in St. Patrick's Cathedral.

MAJOR WORKS

1704	A TALE OF A TUB; THE BATTLE OF THE BOOKS
1724	DRAPIER'S LETTERS
1726	GULLIVER'S TRAVELS
1729	A MODEST PROPOSAL
1739	VERSES ON HIS OWN DEATH

VOLTAIRE

Known by his pen name Voltaire, François-Marie Arouet was the leading French writer of the 18th century. A fanatic believer in personal freedom, he dedicated his life and works to fighting all forms of injustice and intolerance.

François-Marie Arouet was born near Paris, the capital of France, on November 21, 1694. As a schoolboy, he showed great skill in poetry, and at the age of 16, he decided to be a writer.

A REBELLIOUS NATURE

The boy's father, who wanted him to be a lawyer, disapproved of his ambitions. He was so angry that he sent his son to work for the French ambassador at The Hague, in the Netherlands. But the young Arouet stayed in the job for only a few months. He had an affair with a girl, and returned to Paris in disgrace.

His father was furious. He applied for a special order from the king that allowed him to send his son to prison. To make his father happy, François-Marie agreed to study to become a lawyer. But he had still not given up his hope of being a writer. He secretly met a group of poets and began to write.

Seeing that François-Marie was not studying law, his father again threatened to punish him. This time François-

Marie fled to a friend's house in the country. There, he wrote poems, and began his first play, *Oedipus*.

By 1715, his father had become more tolerant of his literary plans, and François-Marie returned to Paris, where he was earning himself a reputation as a poet. He was becoming known to the French government, too. In 1717, the authorities accused him of writing two poems that insulted the king. They threw him in the Bastille prison in Paris.

The conditions of his 11-month stay in jail were not too bad. He was allowed visitors and books, and he had time to write. He now began to use the name that he kept until his death—Voltaire.

Shortly after his release in April 1718, Voltaire staged *Oedipus*. The play was an instant success. The government awarded him a medal and an annual pension in recognition of his genius.

Voltaire, by Nicolas de Largillierre
This picture of the writer in middle age was painted by one of the greatest French portraitists of the early 18th century.

From then on, Voltaire steadily attracted riches and fame. Large audiences flocked to see his plays, and his poems sold well. He was so famous even the king invited him to his wedding.

But Voltaire's excellent connections did not help him when he again got into trouble with the authorities in April 1725. A few months earlier, a young nobleman had insulted him. The writer wanted his revenge, and planned to kill the nobleman. When the police discovered this, they arrested Voltaire and sent him to the Bastille. This time, he was in jail for only two weeks, but on his release he had to leave France.

EXILE FROM FRANCE

Voltaire spent his three-year exile in England. He enjoyed his time there very much. He mastered the English language, and made many friends among the English nobility and literary world.

He admired the English political and religious systems, which he thought were much freer than those in France. He resolved to use his writing to fight the French monarchy and Church.

In April 1729, the French government allowed Voltaire to return to Paris. But he had to flee the capital once more in 1733, when he caused a scandal with his *Philosophical Letters*. The work praised the English government and attacked the French system. The authorities at once condemned the book and ordered the writer's arrest. He escaped to Lorraine, now part of eastern France.

Voltaire spent most of the next 15 years in Lorraine. Although officially a fugitive from the French government,

VOLTAIRE'S CANDIDE

Of Voltaire's hundreds of poems, stories, plays, and political works, one tale has outlasted all the rest.

Many consider *Candide* to be Voltaire's best work. With its wit, vivid characters, and imaginative plot, it is one of the favorite stories of the 18th century.

The tale follows the adventures of a young, innocent boy, Candide (*right*), who travels around Europe and South America. Everywhere he goes, he experiences war, poverty, cannibalism, disease, floods, shipwrecks, and other forms of cruelty and natural disaster. Each situation helps destroy Candide's simple optimism in life.

Voltaire wrote *Candide* as a savage attack on the religious, political, moral, and philosophical

he was still very much in demand as a writer. The French king even asked him to write a play for his son's marriage.

His reputation also spread across Europe. He became a close friend of Frederick the Great, the king of Prussia, now northern Germany. Frederick loved French poetry and thought that Voltaire was the greatest living poet. In 1750, Voltaire accepted an invitation to

This period was one of his most fruitful. He wrote many stories that argued against religious superstition and intolerance, the most famous of which was *Candide*. These works had a great influence on French society by encouraging people to question the authority of the king and the Church.

A TRIUMPHANT RETURN

Despite his success, Voltaire wanted to return to Paris. In spring 1778, after more than 40 years of exile, he decided to take the risk. He was 83 years old, but set off for Paris in good health.

As soon as he arrived in the capital, a stream of visitors called on him. The strain of being on show soon took its toll on Voltaire. He became ill, and his doctors advised him to return home. But he was determined to stay for the opening night of his play, *Irène*, on March 30. The performance was a triumph, and he received an ovation in the theater. The excitement proved too much, however. Voltaire's health rapidly got worse, and on May 30, 1778, he died.

ideas of the day, particularly the belief that no possible world could be better than the actual world in which we live. The world that Candide sees is full of evil. Of all the places he visits, only El Dorado, which is cut off from the outside world by mountains, is an example of the tolerance, justice, liberty, and equality that Voltaire sought.

stay at Frederick's court near Berlin. He spent the next three years there, but left after a quarrel with Frederick.

Still denied entry to France, Voltaire went to Switzerland. Then, in 1759, he moved back to Lorraine. By now, he was very famous. Princes, writers, and philosophers all flocked to see him. He continued to fight injustice, campaigning on behalf of victims of persecution.

MAJOR WORKS

1717	OEDIPUS
1731	HISTORY OF CHARLES XII
1733	PHILOSOPHICAL LETTERS
1753-56	ESSAY ON MANNERS
1759	CANDIDE
1763	TREATISE ON TOLERANCE
1778	IRÈNE

ANTONIO VIVALDI

The musician Vivaldi was also a priest, and his red hair earned him the nickname "The Red Priest." He wrote a huge number of works, but they lay forgotten for almost two centuries after his death.

Antonio Vivaldi was the eldest of six children. He was born on March 4, 1678, in Venice, northern Italy. His father, Giovanni Battista, was a musician at St. Mark's Cathedral, the most important church in the city. He lost no time in teaching the violin to his son, who quickly showed a natural gift.

In his mid-teens, Vivaldi began to train as a priest. He was ordained in 1703. But poor health meant that he had to soon give up some of his duties. This left him more time for his music.

In the fall of 1703, Vivaldi started work as a violin teacher at the Ospedale della Pietà, a charitable home for orphaned and abandoned girls. Some of the girls received a general education, while others also learned how to sing and play instruments. The home had an excellent reputation for music, employing fine teachers and giving concerts each week.

Teaching at the Pietà gave Vivaldi the chance to try out all kinds of different musical styles, and he wrote some of his best pieces for the pupils there. These were performed at the weekly concerts and at various churches in the city. Sometimes, Vivaldi himself played.

Over the next few years, it seems that some of the home's governors opposed having Vivaldi as a teacher for some reason, and he lost his position for two years. By 1716, however, things had changed and he was promoted to the Pietà's master of music.

GROWING FAME

By now, word of Vivaldi's talent had started to spread across Europe, especially after 1705, when he began to publish his work. This meant that his work reached many more people.

By 1718, Vivaldi had staged operas at theaters in Venice and in other cities around northern Italy. Although his operas are seldom performed today, in

Antonio Vivaldi, 1723,
by François Morellon La Cave
This painting by a French artist is thought to be a portrait of the composer in his 40s.

his own day they were very popular. The prince of Mantua awarded the composer an honorary musical title. Vivaldi even gave a special performance for the pope in Rome.

GOSSIP AND SCANDAL

During the 1720s, rumors began to circulate about Vivaldi and a young woman called Anna Giraud. Anna had been the composer's pupil at the Pietà. Soon the rumors turned into scandal when the gossips said that Vivaldi was also involved with Anna's sister. People were shocked that a priest could behave in such a way. The city of Ferrara, northern Italy, which was part of the pope's lands, even forbade Vivaldi from directing an opera there.

THE FOUR SEASONS

In 1725, Vivaldi published *The Contest between Harmony and Invention*. This work became famous all over Europe. Today, the best-known part of the piece is *The Four Seasons*, a musical trip through the year. This was the first example of Vivaldi's "program music"—in which he used sound to conjure up certain feelings or images.

The violin concertos that make up Vivaldi's masterpiece recreate the changing seasons in all their moods and colors, from the brisk, bright celebration of spring, to the bitter winds of winter. Today, it is still one of the most popular pieces of 18th-century music.

Vivaldi was back in Venice from 1726 to 1728, but continued his travels once again in 1729, going to the Austrian capital, Vienna, and possibly to Bohe-

---

VIVALDI AND THE VIOLIN

Vivaldi's works for the violin helped make the instrument the most important of the string family.

By the beginning of the 18th century, when Vivaldi was writing his violin concertos, the violin already had a long history going back more than 200 years. But Vivaldi's determination to create new musical forms helped shape the instrument's future role in the modern orchestra.

In his collection of 12 concertos, *La Stravaganza—The Extraordinary*—of c.1714, Vivaldi divided the string family, which includes the cello, viola, and double bass, as well as the violin, into four sections, and gave a solo part to a single violin. This innovation allowed him to create his famous "program music," in

---

mia, now part of the Czech Republic. All the time the composer was on the move he never lost contact with his duties at the Pietà. He returned there to work whenever he returned to his home city.

RETURN TO VENICE

When he came back to Venice in 1733, Vivaldi settled into composing opera for the Sant'Angelo theater there, as well as

which he used sounds to evoke atmosphere and sensations.

Vivaldi's masterpieces of "program music" are the violin concertos, *The Four Seasons*. In these, a variety of effects represent the times of the year. The *Spring* concerto, for example, uses murmuring strings to suggest gentle breezes and new leaves on trees. *Fall* represents the harvest celebration, with a solo violin evoking drunken men wandering around, falling asleep, and snoring.

working at the Pietà. By 1738, however, the governors of the home had finally had enough of his travels, and fired him.

Despite this, the Pietà asked the composer to write and direct some pieces for a very special occasion. This was a visit by Frederick Christian, crown prince of Saxony-Poland, on March 21, 1740. The visit was a glittering success and, as the music played, all the nearby canals were lit up. The prince took the manuscripts of the music back to his court at Dresden, now in Germany. The collection still survives, and the works are now known as the Dresden concertos.

WANING CAREER

As the years passed, Vivaldi's music became less popular in his home city. The composer, now old and sick, set off for Vienna to see if Charles VI, head of the Holy Roman Empire, would offer him work. The emperor died before Vivaldi reached Vienna, but the composer pressed on in the hope that the new emperor, Francis, would favor him.

In June 1741, Vivaldi finally reached his destination. But he did not have a chance to seek any work. He died of "internal inflammation" on July 28, 1741. He was old, forgotten, and ill when he died. No one now celebrated his work, and he was buried in a pauper's grave. One of the young choirboys at his funeral mass was Joseph Haydn (*see page 82*), who was soon to become a great composer himself.

MAJOR WORKS

1711	HARMONIC INSPIRATION
c.1714	THE EXTRAORDINARY
1714-15	ORLANDO FINTO PAZZO
1716	JUDITHA TRIUMPHANS
1725	THE FOUR SEASONS
1740	THE DRESDEN CONCERTOS

JOHANN SEBASTIAN BACH

Although Bach wrote some astonishingly complex music, his work is still loved by all kinds of people today. In his day, however, most people simply thought of him as a talented organist.

The young Bach was destined to become involved in music in some way. His family was filled with professional musicians. Johann Sebastian was born in Eisenach, Germany, on March 21, 1685. The Protestant Lutheran religion was very important to the people of the town, and religion was to have a great influence on Bach in many ways.

SINGING SCHOLARSHIP

Bach's father, Johann Ambrosius, was a highly regarded church organist. Both he and his wife died while Bach was a boy. The young musician-to-be was adopted and taken in by his elder brother Christoph—also a church organist. Soon he was playing keyboard instruments. By watching the church organ being repaired, the gifted boy also learned valuable lessons about exactly how that instrument worked.

Bach's musical career really began when he was 15. Winning a singing scholarship took him to a town called Lüneberg, to sing in its fine church choir. Here he gained a thorough musical education. Soon, however, his voice changed. No longer able to sing in the choir, Bach switched to playing keyboard instruments with ease, showing particular brilliance at the organ.

The young man then began a lifelong series of jobs as a professional musician. At this time there were plenty of musical posts—Germany was home to all kinds of glittering aristocratic "courts," and its church music was especially impressive. Both church and nobility employed a large number of highly talented singers, musicians, and composers. In 1703, Bach became church organist in the town of Arnstadt.

Bach was stubborn and headstrong from an early age, and things did not go entirely smoothly for him at Arnstadt. On one occasion, he got into trouble for playing for too long in church services.

Johann Sebastian Bach, 1746,
by Elias Gottlob Haussmann
This portrait shows the composer in his early 60s, four years before his death.

His response was to play for a ridiculously short time. On another occasion, he simply abandoned his work in order to walk to a nearby town to hear a recital by a famous Danish organist called Buxtehude.

TO WEIMAR

The year 1707 saw him take up another post—as an organist in Mühlhausen. He also married his cousin, Maria Barbara Bach. Just one year later he moved on again, this time to a post in the Weimar court in eastern Germany. During his nine-year stay there, he wrote some of his finest pieces for organ.

Considering his personality, it is not surprising that Bach's time at Weimar came to an end with an argument. Bach demanded that he be allowed to leave Weimar for the court of Cöthen, and the angry duke of Weimar had him thrown into jail for a short time.

Bach's wish did, however, come true and he found himself working as Prince Leopold's musical director in Cöthen. But by 1723, he had tired of this job, too. The prince now showed less interest in music. As a result, Bach sought new challenges in the city of Leipzig.

Bach's wife had died in 1720, and he had married once again. His second wife was a singer called Anna Magdalena Wilcken. With his two wives, Bach had a total of 20 children.

Bach lived in Leipzig for the rest of his life. This was a bustling and cultural city, filled with music. Bach was appointed organist of St. Thomas's Church, which was an important post. He was also made the city's music director. In

---

BACH AND THE ORGAN

The composer most closely linked with the organ was Bach, who wrote nearly 250 works for the instrument.

Bach's contemporary, Wolfgang Amadeus Mozart (*see page 86*), described the organ (*right*) as "the king of musical instruments" because of its large size. The oldest of all keyboard instruments, it dates back to the third century B.C.. Since then, all models have been made up of the same basic elements.

The sound an organ produces is made by air resonating in pipes. It involves air being blown mechanically through the pipes by way of one or more keyboards, or manuals. Each rank of pipes has its own characteristic tone, which usually imitates that of a wind instrument.

---

this role, he was in charge of church and civic music across the city, composing pieces for all kinds of occasions.

Bach had, in fact, been lucky to get this prestigious job, especially as most people regarded him as an organist rather than a composer. Luckily for him, there was no better candidate around. This situation did not, however, alter Bach's arrogant attitude. He quarreled

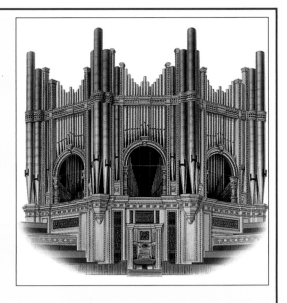

MAJOR WORKS

1721	THE BRANDENBURG CONCERTOS
1722	THE WELL-TEMPERED CLAVIER
1729	ST. MATTHEW PASSION
1734	CHRISTMAS ORATORIO
1749	THE ART OF THE FUGUE

The golden age of the organ was the 18th century, by which time it was mainly used as a church instrument. Bach was famous not only as an organ player, but also as an expert designer and builder of the instrument. He also wrote a large number of compositions for the organ. They reveal his extraordinary versatility. Some are highly dramatic pieces, designed to show off the skills of the player, while others are solemn, hymnlike works.

with Leipzig's councillors, and was often criticized for ignoring his duties.

Bach was also famous for being cheap. When a relative sent him some wine as a gift, he complained that some had been spilled. He was also unhappy at having to pay delivery charges, and asked his relative to send no more gifts.

While Bach wrote most of his music for the organ, he also wrote many pieces to be sung in church, such as his *St. Matthew Passion*, Many people consider this to be one of his finest works. Yet when it was first performed, in around 1729, some of the public criticized it for being too unusual.

Forever pushing forward musical barriers, Bach is especially famous for his pioneering work with counterpoint—weaving two or more lines of melody together—and many consider his *The Art of the Fugue* to be a supreme masterpiece of this technique. The composer also wrote more than 200 cantatas—works for voices and orchestras—on religious subjects, and he is credited with bringing an elaborate and flamboyant style of music known as Baroque—which began in around 1600—to its peak.

Bach died in Leipzig, after a stroke, on July 28, 1750. The fashion for Baroque music was dying and a simpler style was taking over. Bach's music was forgotten until the 1800s, when it saw somewhat of a revival. Ever since then, Bach's reputation as a true genius has never faded.

GEORGE FRIDERIC HANDEL

Best known today for his music for special occasions and his choral works, the German-born Handel was responsible during his lifetime for making Italian-style opera popular in London, his adopted home.

George Frideric Handel was born in Halle, Germany, on February 23, 1685. His father, Georg, who was a highly respected barber and surgeon, was 63 when George was born. He was set in his ways and wanted his son to follow a steady career as a lawyer. When George showed an interest in music, he was not happy; he would not even allow him to own a musical instrument. The young Handel was stubborn, however. He smuggled a clavichord—an early type of piano—into the house and practiced in secret.

Handel's father must have finally recognized his son's musical gift. When George was a teenager, he allowed him to have music lessons with Friedrich Zachow, the organist at the local church.

By the age of 17, in 1702, he was a talented organ and harpsichord player, and had composed several pieces of music. Nonetheless, that same year he began to study law at Halle University, while also playing as an organist at a nearby church. Music won out at last.

Handel left his law studies behind in 1703 to move to the lively city of Hamburg. Here, he taught music, and also played harpsichord and violin in the orchestra of the Hamburg Opera.

WORKING IN THE OPERA

By the time Handel was 21, he had already seen three of his operas performed. The first one, *Almira*, was considered a great success.

In 1705, Handel left for the Italian city of Florence. He spent three years in the city, soaking up musical styles and working as a musician in the household of the Marquis Francesco Ruspoli. He wrote cantatas for the marquis's weekly concerts, as well as many pieces of church music.

By now, the young composer was making important contacts all over Italy, and receiving great praise

George Frideric Handel, by Philip Mercier **Mercier, a French artist who spent most of his career in England, shows Handel working on a new composition.**

wherever he went. One of the people he met was Prince Ernst August of Hanover, in Germany. The prince's brother was Georg Ludwig, the elector, or ruler, of Hanover, who later became King George I of England. Prince Ernst was eager for the composer to visit his country. So, in 1710, Handel arrived in Hanover and became the elector's musical director. Apart from a period in England, Handel spent the next two years writing music for Georg Ludwig.

A MOVE TO LONDON

Handel had enjoyed his time in England, and in late 1712, he moved there permanently. He had good connections in London, and was soon performing at the court of Queen Anne. When she died, in 1714, Georg Ludwig became King George I and appointed Handel master of royal music. He composed the *Water Music* (1717) for one of the king's boating parties. In 1727, Handel wrote some pieces for the coronation of the next king, George II. One of these, *Zadok the Priest*, has been performed at every British coronation since.

Many of Handel's contemporaries left accounts of his life in London. He was a big, imposing man with a huge appetite. He was impatient and had a short temper, but he could also be witty and wonderful company.

Handel devoted much of his energy in London to developing Italian-style opera. He also helped to create the city's first permanent opera house, the Royal Academy of Music. Appointed musical director of the academy, Handel wrote several operas to be performed there.

THE CLAVICHORD

Developed in the 14th century, the clavichord was a precursor of the modern piano.

The clavichord (*right*), the instrument on which Handel secretly learned to play music, was an early kind of keyboard instrument. By the 18th century, it had become the most important instrument in domestic use.

The clavichord was too soft in tone to be played effectively in public. And since it was cheaper and smaller than the harpsichord, more people could afford to have one in their homes.

The clavichord was more expressive than the harpsichord. It could sustain notes and graduate its volume. Rather than being plucked, the strings were instead hit by a tangent—a

After the academy went bankrupt, in 1728, Handel continued to stage his operas at other theaters. But they were failures. At the same time, Handel also became partly paralyzed. But these problems did not deter him. Instead of writing Italian operas, he started to produce English oratorios—works for choirs and orchestras—hoping that these would be more popular.

brass blade—at the end of the key. The clavichord did not require as many strings as it had keys, since several tangents could hit the same string at different places. This factor contributed greatly to its small size, portability, and easy tuning.

Some versions of the clavichord—known as pedal clavichords—were fitted with pedals and used as practice instruments by organists. Thus, it was an ideal instrument for Handel to practice on and learn the variety of keyboard skills that helped make his name.

These works were not greeted with great enthusiasm either, and Handel's career continued to fail. But success came once again when he visited Ireland in 1741. Here, he wrote his great *Messiah* oratorio. The first performance, in Dublin on April 13, 1742, was a triumph.

Back in England, however, the *Messiah* was not as popular—English audiences did not like the idea of a religious work being performed in an ordinary theater rather than in a church.

THE LAST YEARS

In 1746, the country's mood changed. That year, at the Battle of Culloden, English forces put down a Scottish uprising, part of an attempt to seize the English throne. As part of the celebrations following the victory, Handel wrote his *Occasional Oratorio*.

Two years later, the War of the Austrian Succession, in which England had been fighting, came to an end. To celebrate, the king asked Handel to compose some music to accompany a royal fireworks display. His *Music for the Royal Fireworks* became one of his best-known works.

Now over 60, Handel worked less and less. In 1751, he began to go blind. By 1759, his health was very poor. Just a few days after staging his final series of oratorios, Handel died. Some 3,000 people attended his funeral.

MAJOR WORKS

1705	ALMIRA
1708	LA RESURREZIONE
1717	WATER MUSIC
1727	ZADOK THE PRIEST
1742	MESSIAH
1746	OCCASIONAL ORATORIO
1749	MUSIC FOR THE ROYAL FIREWORKS

JOSEPH HAYDN

Celebrated as a composer of genius during his lifetime, Haydn was a central figure in the growth of the Classical style. Although successful in all forms of instrumental music, he is considered the father of the symphony.

Joseph Haydn was born in 1732 in Rohrau, a small town close to Austria's border with Hungary. He was the second of 12 children, only six of whom reached adulthood. As a boy, Haydn showed musical talent, delighting his family with his beautiful singing.

SCHOOL IN HAINBURG

In 1738, when Joseph was just six years old, his parents sent him away to study in Hainburg. He was put into the care of a distant relative called Johann Mathias Franck, who was the town's schoolmaster and organist. Franck was not a kind man, and he treated his pupils harshly, often beating them. But he encouraged Haydn's gift for singing and taught him to play several instruments.

Two years later, Haydn's musical education received another boost. The choirmaster of St. Stephen's Cathedral in Vienna, the capital of Austria, heard him sing and took him into the choir. Soon, Haydn was singing in cathedral services and at the Austrian emperor's

court. But once his voice changed, he was of no further use to the choirmaster, who looked for an excuse to get rid of him. When the mischievous Haydn cut off another chorister's pigtail in 1749, the choirmaster threw him out onto the streets of Vienna.

The penniless 18-year-old Haydn, close to starvation, roamed the capital. By chance, he met a music teacher called Michael Spangler, who invited him to share his lodgings. Soon, Haydn started to scrape a living from teaching, playing, and composing. His fortunes changed when he met an Italian composer, Nicola Porpora, who took the struggling musician on as his accompanist. Working for Porpora, Haydn learned about composing, and met important, cultured people.

Haydn's new contacts made all the difference. An Austrian aristocrat, Karl

Portrait of Joseph Haydn, 1792, by Thomas Hardy
This painting shows the composer at the age of 60.

Joseph von Fürnberg, asked Haydn to perform at his house. The young man wrote his first string quartets here.

He also met Count von Morzin of Bohemia—now in the Czech Republic—who made Haydn his musical director. Word of the young composer's talents now started to spread throughout the Austrian Empire.

In 1760, Haydn married Maria Anna Keller. But the couple had nothing at all in common. Maria Anna even used Haydn's manuscripts to line her pastry tins. Haydn buried himself in his work.

A NEW START

In 1761, Count von Morzin disbanded his orchestra. But Haydn soon found a new job as assistant musical director for Prince Paul Anton Esterházy, a wealthy and influential Austrian nobleman.

In 1762, Prince Paul died and his brother, Nikolaus, became head of the family. This was the start of a golden age for Haydn. Nikolaus was a highly cultured man and, in 1766, he promoted Haydn to musical director. That year he moved his court to a new palace in Hungary. The sumptuous palace, known as Eszterháza, had its own opera house, where Haydn staged several operas.

SPREADING REPUTATION

During the 1770s, Haydn wrote a great deal and started to have his works published by a Viennese publisher. Their publication enhanced his reputation throughout Europe and he became an international celebrity.

In around 1781, Haydn met the great Austrian composer Wolfgang Amadeus

---

HAYDN AT ESZTERHÁZA

For almost 30 years, Haydn's career was centered on a luxurious palace in Hungary.

In 1766, Prince Nikolaus Esterházy made Haydn his musical director. The same year, Nikolaus established his court at the splendid Eszterháza palace at Süttör, in Hungary.

Two of the new facilities at Eszterháza were a marionette theater and an opera house. For both of these places, Haydn created successful and original works. He wrote most of these for special occasions, such as marriages and royal visits. *L'incontro improvviso* (*above right*), for example, was first performed in 1775, when the Austrian Archduke Ferdinand visited Eszterháza.

Mozart (*see page 86*), who became a close friend. In 1790, Prince Nikolaus died, and his son Anton became head of the family. Anton was not a musical man and he disbanded the orchestra, although he awarded Haydn an excellent pension for his long, faithful service. Haydn now returned to Vienna.

In the winter of 1790, Haydn left for England. He had been invited to London

During his time at the palace, Haydn experimented with musical forms, combining instruments to invent new effects. In particular, he produced highly expressive symphonies. Unlike earlier Baroque music, which was exuberant and complex, Haydn's works had clear, uncomplicated melodies.

Haydn's style reflected the movement known as Neoclassicism, which sought to recreate the pure, simple, and harmonious balance of ancient art. Haydn's classical approach helped him produce music that was not too heavy, but light and easy for the audience to follow.

to conduct a season of concerts that included some new works of his own.

Haydn was an instant hit, sought by royalty and honored everywhere. One of his most successful London works was *Symphony No. 94: The Surprise*. Because of the wonderful reception, Haydn stayed in England for longer than he had originally intended, but in 1792, he headed back to Vienna.

Haydn missed the excitement of London and, in 1794, he returned. Now in his early 60s, he was even more of a success than before. King George III offered him a suite in Windsor Castle. But Haydn was 63 years old and wanted to spend his final years in his homeland.

A RETURN TO VIENNA

In 1795, Haydn set off for Vienna again, once more to take up the position of musical director to the Esterházy family, which had asked the composer to reform the court orchestra and choir. Haydn's greatest work from these final years was his oratorio—a work for voices and orchestra—*The Creation*.

By 1809, Haydn was in very poor health. Just before his death, French troops occupied Vienna. The composer was so famous that the French emperor, Napoleon Bonaparte, placed a guard of honor outside his door so that troops would not harm him. He died on May 31, 1809.

MAJOR WORKS

1759	SYMPHONY NO. 1
1764	SYMPHONY NO. 22: THE PHILOSOPHER
1791	SYMPHONY NO. 94: THE SURPRISE
1793	VARIATIONS IN F MINOR
1794	SYMPHONY NO. 101: THE CLOCK; SYMPHONY NO. 104: THE LONDON
1798	THE CREATION

WOLFGANG AMADEUS
MOZART

A child-star across Europe by the age of ten, Mozart astonished people everywhere with his incredible talent for playing the violin and piano. Yet life did not always go smoothly for this temperamental genius.

Wolfgang Amadeus Mozart's remarkable childhood began in 1756, in the town of Salzburg, Austria. He was encouraged to play music from an early age. His father, Leopold, was a violinist in the orchestra of Count von Schrattenbach, the Prince-Archbishop of Salzburg. Mozart was educated at home, along with his older sister Nannerl, who was also musically gifted.

THE BOY GENIUS

It was soon clear that Mozart was a genius. Not only was he brilliant at mathematics and languages, but his musical gift was amazing. By the time he was four years old, he was able to play any instrument he could lay his hands on. At the age of five, Mozart stunned his father when he played six string trios perfectly on his small violin. Leopold immediately set about arranging for his little son to make a grand tour of Europe.

During the early 1760s, the Mozart family began an exhausting series of tours across Europe that lasted about ten years. They traveled through Germany, Belgium, France, England, and Italy. Wherever they went, Mozart displayed his skill to nobility and royalty, performing at the grand houses and courts of Europe, including the French palace of Versailles. While he was in France, Mozart wrote two sonatas that became his first published works.

IMPRESSING THE WORLD

Everyone was astonished by the boy's gifts. Mozart played for the Austrian emperor, who called him "my little wizard." In London, King George III set Mozart several difficult tests on the keyboard—the boy passed them all easily. One person he played for could not believe he was not even ten years old, and asked for a copy of his birth certificate to be sent from Salzburg.

Wolfgang Amadeus Mozart
This undated portrait shows the young composer seated at a clavichord. The name of the artist is not known.

Mozart and his sister paid a large price for the fame that made them grow up too fast. The constant traveling weakened their health, and both became very ill with typhoid. Mozart grew up into a moody young man. He swung dramatically between being too serious for his age and breaking out suddenly into hysterical laughter or tears. When he was an adult, he was known for his childish behavior, including a love of practical jokes, that lasted all his life.

CONTINUED SUCCESS

Between about 1766 and 1769, the Mozarts divided their time between Vienna and Salzburg. Mozart continued to compose, and Leopold's employer, Count von Schrattenbach, made the boy an honorary concertmaster, at the age of just 13.

In 1771, the Mozarts returned to Salzburg after a tour of Italy to discover that von Schrattenbach had died. The count had always been extremely reasonable about all of Leopold's trips away. But his new employer, Count Colloredo, was not so understanding. He was determined that the young Amadeus should take his duties as concertmaster more seriously.

A TROUBLED TIME

Mozart continued to compose—church music, operas, violin concertos, and his first concerto for piano. Keyboard and chamber music—for small ensembles of instruments and/or voices—seemed to flow from his pen with almost no effort at all. He soon became restless again, however, and asked Colloredo for

THE MAGIC FLUTE

A dramatic, ambitious, and highly imaginative work, *The Magic Flute* still charms audiences today.

An opera in two acts, *The Magic Flute* is one of Mozart's most popular works. The story is set in ancient Egypt. Prince Tamino falls in love with Pamina, daughter of the evil Queen of the Night. Tamino has to pass a series of tests, with the help of a magic flute, before the couple's love can triumph over darkness.

The opera is full of fantastical figures, such as Papageno, the bird-man (*above right*), various spirits, and the evil Moor. The settings are also exotic, from mountains and rocky valleys to temples and moonlit gardens.

The Magic Flute was commissioned by Mozart's close

time off to visit Paris. The count refused, and Mozart lost his job.

Therefore, at 21, Mozart decided to set out on tour alone in search of fame and fortune. His father did not want him to go alone, so the young man's mother, Anna Maria, went with him. Things did not go well in Paris. Mozart was a success but found it hard to get paid work. And Anna Maria was desperately

friend, Emanuel Schikaneder, an actor-manager. Schikaneder knew how to make people flock to his productions by using spectacular sets and fantastic stories. When the opera opened in Vienna in 1791, the glorious music and wonderful spectacle captivated the audience.

resigned. This was a troubled period of the composer's life. He did succeed in writing his opera, *Idomeneo*, however.

A HAPPY MARRIAGE

Life now began to improve for Mozart. He moved to Vienna in 1781, and took lodgings with a family called the Webers. Some time earlier, Mozart had fallen in love with Aloysia Weber, but she was now married. He turned his attentions to her younger sister Constanze, who was a singer, and the two married in 1782. Leopold disapproved of the match, as he thought that his son had married beneath him, but it seems that it was a happy marriage. The

> "The majority of spectators will enjoy it; the initiated will understand its higher meaning."
> (German poet Goethe on *The Magic Flute*)

homesick. In July 1777, she fell ill with fever and died suddenly. Her devastated son wandered the streets of Paris, wondering how he could break the news to his father.

Depressed and disillusioned, Mozart finally returned home to Salzburg, and was taken on once more by Count Colloredo. He stayed for three years, but was so unhappy and restless that he

couple had six children, only two of whom survived beyond childhood.

This was a successful time in the composer's life. He wrote the first of a series of 12 piano concertos as well as his great C minor mass, and his opera, *The Abduction from the Seraglio*, was performed for the first time.

Mozart also met the highly respected Austrian composer, Joseph Haydn (*see*

Set design for The Magic Flute, 1818, by Simon Quaglio
This colorful design was produced for the performance of Mozart's opera in Munich on November 27, 1818.

page 82), around this time. Haydn, who was almost 25 years older than Mozart, was one of his greatest admirers.

Then a shadow fell over the young composer's life. Although Mozart was paid a salary by the Austrian emperor,

the emperor's musical director seemed to have much more influence at court. This musical director was a well-respected composer called Antonio Salieri, who was bitterly jealous of the new talent. When Mozart died, there were even rumors that Salieri had poisoned him, although no proof of this has ever been found.

Mozart's last five years were very productive. He wrote some of his most popular operas—*The Marriage of Figaro* in 1786, *Don Giovanni* in 1787 and *Così fan tutte* (All Women are Like That) in 1790. There were other works, too. He wrote his elegant work for strings, *A Little Night Music*, in 1787, and this is still a favorite today. He also created piano concertos that pushed forward what it was possible to do in that form of music, as well as three symphonies, which showed a whole range of emotions.

FIGHTING ILLNESS

Despite the success of many of his later works, Mozart made very little money from them. Now illness came to Mozart and his wife. Constanze needed to take expensive cures that they could not afford, and Mozart started to suffer from kidney disease. Yet despite the fact that he was constantly fighting symptoms such as headaches and rheumatism, Mozart continued to write music at great speed.

THE FINAL YEAR

The year 1791 was the last of the composer's life. He produced an opera called *The Magic Flute*, which was a dramatic mixture of serious themes and comedy. It is a work welded together out of three different traditions: grand opera, religious music, and comedy. Mozart, desperate for money, waited anxiously for the public's response. But his work was not successful at first, and this, combined with money problems and poor health, drove Mozart closer to death. Gradually, however, *The Magic Flute* soared to widespread success. The composer would live just long enough to see it acclaimed.

DEATH AND DEBT

When a messenger arrived to commission a funeral mass from him, Mozart took this as a sign of his own death, and worked nonstop to complete it. It was still unfinished, however, when he died, on December 5, 1791.

As an imperial decree had gone out saying that no large gatherings or expensive funerals were to take place, this great genius was buried in an unmarked pauper's grave. He left behind huge debts, most of which Constanze repaid after his death, largely by the sale of his manuscripts.

MAJOR WORKS

1768	LA FINTA SEMPLICE
1782	THE ABDUCTION FROM THE SERAGLIO
1782-85	"HAYDN" STRING QUARTETS
1786	THE MARRIAGE OF FIGARO
1787	DON GIOVANNI; A LITTLE NIGHT MUSIC
1788	SYMPHONY IN G MINOR
1790	COSÌ FAN TUTTE
1791	THE MAGIC FLUTE; REQUIEM MASS

GLOSSARY

academy A society formed to advance the practice of art, literature, or music.

aria A musical composition for a solo singer with orchestral accompaniment, particularly associated with operas and oratorios.

Baroque The prevalent style of European art in the 17th century, in which the artist attempted to overwhelm the senses and the emotions of the viewer, reader, or listener by means of elaborate and theatrical artistic forms.

canvas A firm, closely woven cloth on which an artist paints a picture.

classical art The art of ancient Greece and Rome. Sometimes called antique, or ancient, art.

Classicism The styles of ancient Greek and Roman art and literature. Also refers to the work of later artists, writers, and composers who followed the classical rules of restraint, harmony, and balance.

commission An order received by an artist, writer, or composer from a patron to produce a work of art, literature, or music.

composition The arrangement or organization of the various elements of a work of art, literature, or music.

concerto In the 17th century, the term could apply to any work combining voices and instruments; later it came to mean an instrumental work, usually in three movements.

counterpoint A musical term referring to the simultaneous combination of two or more independent melodies.

engraving A method of making prints by cutting lines or dots into a hard surface, usually a metal plate.

fêtes galantes A kind of early-18th-century French painting in which people are shown amusing themselves in an outdoor setting.

history painting A kind of painting that shows historical, religious, mythological, or literary subjects depicted in an impressive manner.

landscape A kind of painting showing a view of natural scenery, such as mountains or forests.

medium Term used to describe the various methods and materials of the artist, such as oil paint on canvas, or watercolor.

mythology A collection of stories about the gods or legendary heroes of a particular people.

narrative The representation in art or literature of a story or event.

Neoclassicism The predominant artistic movement in Europe in the late 18th and early 19th centuries. It was characterized by a revival of the ideals of classical art, in an attempt to recapture the heroic spirit of ancient Greece and Rome.

occasional music Music composed for a specific occasion or event.

opera A dramatic musical work, first developed in late-16th-century Italy, in which the characters sing the text, accompanied by an orchestra.

oratorio A large-scale concert work for solo singers, chorus, and orchestra.

patron A person or organization that asks an artist, writer, or composer to create a work of art, literature, or music. Usually the patron pays for the work.

portrait A drawing, painting, or sculpture that gives a likeness of a person and often provides an insight into his or her personality.

print A picture produced by pressing a piece of paper against a variety of inked surfaces, including engraved metal plates and wooden blocks.

There are several different methods of making prints, including engraving.

program music Music inspired by, or intended to illustrate or evoke, something outside of music—a picture, a story, a person, etc.

quartet A musical piece usually composed for four string instruments or four singers.

Rococo A French style of art and architecture that began around 1700, and then spread throughout Europe. It was characterized by lightness, grace, and elegance.

satire The use of wit, irony, or sarcasm to expose human folly and vices to ridicule and contempt.

sitter A person who has his or her portrait produced by an artist.

sketch A rough or quick version of a picture, often produced as a trial-run for a more finished work.

still life A drawing or painting of objects that cannot move by themselves, such as fruit or flowers.

style The distinctive appearance of a particular artist, writer, or composer's work of art.

symphony A serious orchestral work with several movements (often four) of different tempos, or speeds, and contrasting expressive qualities.

FURTHER READING

Banfield, Susan. *The Rights of Man, the Reign of Terror: The Story of the French Revolution*. HarperCollins Children's, 1990

Chapman, Laura. *Art: Images and Ideas*, "Discover Art" series. Davis Pubns., Inc., 1992

Copland, Aaron. *What to Listen for in Music*. NAL/Dutton, 1989

Defoe, Daniel. *Robinson Crusoe*. Puffin Books, 1995

Janson, H.W. *The History of Art*. Abrams, 1995 (standard reference)

The New Grove Dictionary of Music and Musicians. Grove's Dictionaries of Music, 1980 (standard reference)

Patton, Barbara W. *Introducing Johann Sebastian Bach*, "Introducing the Composers" series. Soundboard Books, 1992

Reyero, Carlos. *The Key to Art from Romanticism to Impressionism*, "Key to Art Books." Lerner Group, 1990

Swortzell, Lowell. *Gulliver's Travels*. Anchorage Press, 1992

Thompson, Wendy. *Joseph Haydn*, "Composer's World" series. Viking Children's, 1991
——— *Wolfgang Amadeus Mozart*, "Composer's World" series. Viking Children's, 1991

Triado, Juan-Ramon. *The Key to Baroque Art*. Lerner Group, 1990

INDEX